COME WITH ME

Daily Living with a
New Monastic Rule of Life

Wendy J. Miller

Introduction

This book is not just a text to be read. Rather, you are invited on a journey—an adventure of sorts. As you begin this journey, you may wonder where it will take you, and how you will get there.

The followers of John the Baptist – whom John called to follow Jesus – also wondered, also carried questions with them.

> The next day John again was standing with two of his disciples, and as he watched Jesus walk by, he exclaimed, "Look, here is the Lamb of God!" The two disciples heard him say this, and they followed Jesus. When Jesus turned and saw them following, he said to them, "What are you looking for?" They said to him, "Rabbi . . . where are you staying?" He said to them, "Come and see." (John 1:25-39)[1]

Jesus asks us the same question.

---

[1] All scripture quotations are from The New Revised Standard Version, or author's paraphrase when noted.

As you pause and reflect on the journey you are beginning, listen to Jesus asking you that question.

"What are you looking for?"

How do you reply? Journal your thoughts in the space below.

Jesus invites us to "come and see." However, this is not a virtual, self-guided tour. Jesus also says things like, "Come with me." And "Listen to me."

> Jesus came to Galilee, proclaiming the good news of God, and saying, "The time is fulfilled, and the kingdom of God has come near; repent (turn around, turn from the life that is tiring, constricted, based on accumulation and production) and believe in the good news."
> As Jesus passed along the Sea of Galilee, he saw Simon and his brother Andrew casting a net into the sea – for they were fishermen. And Jesus said to them, "Follow me and I will make you fish for people." (Mark 1:14 – 17)

Mark's gospel invites us to walk further into the gospel story and join these disciples as they return to their work in Capernaum in Galilee after their first encounter with Jesus in Jerusalem.

We find ourselves on the shores of Lake Galilee, wading barefoot into the stony shallows, and watching as these fishermen throw great circles of nets out into the water. As we watch these men fishing we become aware that we are not alone. Jesus joins us as we wait and watch.

In such quiet ways God comes alongside us in the daily work, our common routine. We are often unaware of this divine presence, even as these disciples are unaware that this is the Son of God standing knee-deep in the lake alongside them. However, they have begun to pin their hopes on Jesus as the Messiah. So when he says, "Follow me and I will make you fish for people," they are ready to give him their loyalty, and even though they do not fully understand the meaning of Jesus' call, they leave their nets and follow him (Mark 1:18).

Jesus is still calling us today: "Follow me." "Come with me."

The disciples discover that being with Jesus becomes a complete life-changer for those who go with him, a life change neither they nor we expect.

God comes and lives among us – in Jesus. The Creator God who has spoken all of creation--earth, sea, sky, and all of life into being--now walks among us in Jesus. Peter offers Jesus lodging at his house in Capernaum, a town that hugs the shore of the Sea of Galilee (Mark 1:14, 21, 29). We too are invited into the story where we soon realize that Jesus is no ordinary houseguest. He tells stories at table and invites children into the circle of adult conversation to receive a blessing. Jesus has a way of reminding high-minded grownups that children are our teachers when it comes to knowing who God is and what God is about. Children are leaders when it comes to entering the kingdom of heaven – the home for which we long.

Simon Peter remembers how Jesus healed his mother-in-law who was in bed with a fever. Jesus had also showed his authority in the synagogue that day, ordering an unclean spirit to leave a man who began shouting in the middle of a sermon. Those standing by were astounded at his teaching, and "that evening at sundown, they brought to him all who were sick or possessed with demons. And the whole city gathered around the door" at Simon's house (Mark 1:32-33).

As we remain within the gospel story, listening, we realize that we may try to give Jesus a place to stay in a spare room, but the Lord of the universe is not content to be a quiet, unobtrusive guest. Soon he will attract people we would rather not touch or be seen with – the lepers of society who come with requests: "If you choose, you can make me clean." Jesus moved with pity, stretches out his hand to touch, saying, "I do choose. Be made clean! (Mark 1:40-44). Then he begins explaining how these folks who have been legally banned from any physical contact –at table, among family, in the market place, at worship, at weddings, or family festivities are now to be a part of our family circle! People will dismantle the protective roof of our house in order to get closer to this Jesus within for they and their friends need healing too (Mark 2:1-12).

We discover that Jesus relates to women with the power of respect and tenderness. He declares that they are full members of the household of God, and includes women among those he commissions for missional ministry. For men he models the greatness of servanthood; and if Jesus criticizes, he speaks out against "the very premises on which domination is based: the right of some to lord it over others by means of power, wealth, shaming, or titles."[2]

Some people react against Jesus. They say he goes too far, and they want him out of the way (Mark 3:6). But in our hearts we know we need his message, and not just we, but the persons around us, the towns, the cities, the nations. And when he says, "Come with me," we go with him -- in spite of our fear and resistance as Jesus forthrightly recites a list of all the evil and unhealed wounds that we thought we had hidden safely in the basement of our heart-house: "From [your] heart come the evil ideas which lead [you] to kill, commit adultery, and do other immoral things: to rob, lie, and slander others"
(Matthew 15:29, TEV).

Now that Jesus has seen behind the respectable paint-work and knows what goes on behind closed doors, we are astonished that he stays with us, and wants us around with him. Instead he says that he wants to make his home with us, basement and all; and we know we are in the presence of a love we cannot fathom. It is this Jesus who says to us: "Come with me." As we stay with this Jesus, we are forever changed: our lives become re-patterned and re-ordered around God and God's purposes in the world. The journey becomes a pilgrimage, which leads into missional engagement.

---

[2] Walter Wink. "The Kingdom: God's Domination-Free Order," *Weavings: A Journal of the Christian Spiritual Life* (January/February 1995):12; Quoted in Miller, Wendy. *Invitation to Presence: A Guide to Spiritual Disciplines* Upper Room Books, 1995, 4.

Design

COME WITH ME is designed to be a guide and a workbook, giving you the kind of map that can help with the inward and the outward journey. In its pages you will find guidance as you explore the landscape of your own life and soul, and as you engage with an outward journey, encountering people you may have never met or spent time with before--all kinds of people. That is the way of Jesus, tending our inner being, even as we are engaging with other people, some of whom others criticize, do not want to be with, or do not have time for. The following sections in each chapter are designed to companion you on this inward and outward pilgrimage:

Guide for the Journey Inward

Over many centuries we have lost our way, and avoid entering into the territory of the soul – our own heart and being. Hence we are unsure how to attend to the soul journey of another. But the Spirit of God is at work, brooding over the anxious waters of our inner being, and awakening a hunger for God, for the Spirit, for something "more" than what the world demands that we buy, accumulate, or accomplish.

COME WITH ME takes us on an inward journey. Guidance will be given as you learn to walk the pathways of your soul, and to grow in your relationship with God. The emphasis will be on formation, rather than gathering information; on being rather than doing.

As you read and prayerfully reflect, have your bible and your journal --written or on computer--at hand.

Guide for the Outward Journey

Along with other journey partners, you will be traveling with persons who, like you, are feeling a need to learn how to walk both the inward and outward journey of emergence in the church "wherever 2 or 3 are gathered" in Christ's name – finding where the Spirit of Christ is present and at work in unlikely places, among all kinds of people. "Come with me" takes us out, beyond our lines of comfort or expectation – into "beyond the border" territory. This book comes alongside as a guide as you travel – for your own journey, and for those you walk with on pilgrimage.

Guide for Daily Living with a New Monastic Rule of Life

As you discern where God is calling you to attend to a "Calcutta"[3] within your local community, you will be living into a new monastic rule of life. Rather than being just words on a page, the new monastic rule speaks into what is to be embodied in who we are and what we do, individually, and as a group--tending the emergence of missional communities that God will bring into being as we "come and see" where Jesus lives.

Guidance from others who have walked this inward and outward missional and monastic path:

We do not travel alone. Other pilgrims—past and present--walk with us. As you read what these fellow travelers have written, imagine yourself sitting down for conversation with them, or walking the streets of your own Calcutta with them. Listen to what they are sharing with you. Note your conversation with them in your journal as we walk through this guide together.

---

[3] Shane Claiborne remembers his conversations with Mother Teresa, while he was living and working in Calcutta, India, caring for lepers. Shane was wondering about staying there, permanently. But Mother Theresa replied: "Calcuttas are everywhere, if only we have eyes to see." He knew he needed to find his own "Calcutta" and serve there. See: Claiborne, Shane. *Irresistible Revolution: Living as an Ordinary Radical.* Grand Rapids: Zondervan, 2006) 89.

For Your Reflection

Rather than being a "fast read" in order to "get information," this workbook invites you into the slower pilgrim pathway of reading for formation, the kind of attentiveness that allows ourselves to be read. Instead of mastering the text, we allow the God who is within and behind the text to help us to see and hear what God is attending to in our lives. The "For Your Reflection" questions are there to help you to pause and to prayerfully reflect on your own life and ministry experience. You may respond in the spaces offered, or in your journal of choice.

Gathering a small group of journey partners

When Jesus says, "Come with me," he is calling first a small group, and later larger groups of followers, to go with him, to become journey partners on this inward and outward path. This kind of formational trek is best walked with others. Take some time to prayerfully consider whom you might invite, whom you would ask to "Come with me."[4]

Write their names below, look up their phone numbers and email addresses, and add that information alongside their names. Be in prayer about the persons you have listed, and ask God to guide you as you begin a conversation with them. A helpful way to begin is to invite these persons over for a simple meal and conversation – a conversation about a new kind of personal, formational, community, and missional venture. Have copies of this book available for your resource and for them to see and read. You will also find it helpful to have a copy of *Missional. Monastic. Mainline.*

---

[4] See further guidance for gathering a lead team in Heath, Elaine A. and Larry Duggins, *Missional. Monastic. Mainline: A Guide to Starting Missional Micro-Communities in Historically Mainline Traditions.* Cascade Books, 2014. Ch.8 "Gathering a Lead Team for a Missional Community."

Possible Journey Partners

Explain your interest and how you are praying for God's guidance as you invite a small group to walk with you in this formative and missional venture.

Allow time for responses, questions, ideas. Make a note of the conversation. Then discuss when you will meet again, and who would like to host. Meeting once every two weeks can be a sustaining rhythm.

Close with prayers of thanksgiving, some silence, and then a blessing.

1

Healing What is Broken

What does Jesus have in mind when he says, "Come with me; follow me"? Simon Peter, his brother Andrew, and the others who hear Jesus' call and turn to follow him discover only gradually what Jesus is truly about. We will learn with them that we are walking on a journey of the heart, as well as a journey outward into the world around us. How does Jesus help us discover the way inward and the way outward? Come and see!

As we come we bring our longings, hopes and expectations (known and unknown) with us. [5]

---

[5] Elaine Heath and Scott Kisker speak to these longings in their book, *Longing for Spring: A New Vision for Wesleyan Community.* Cascade Books, 2010.

Expectations

The gospel narrators also come with expectations. They expect Jesus to reclaim the monarchy, to be installed on the throne of David, and to restore the political fortunes of Israel – and their personal fortunes along with him. This pre-understanding of the early disciples arises out of their national and religious story (Luke 24:19-21; Acts 1:6-7).

Any expectations we bring with us on this journey of being with Jesus, emerge out of how the world works in which we live; our own history. The world's system has formed us, taught us its rules, its ways of engagement: how to get an education, what is important to learn, which colleges and graduate schools to attend, how to get a job – a successful job, and how to re-train ourselves if that job doesn't last. The culture in which we live teaches us how to relate, how to make friends and influence people, which car to drive, what clothes to wear, and what part of the town or city to live in. If we have been "raised" in the church, then there is another set of rules – written, spoken, and unspoken – to live by.

Many of these values can be life-giving, and life-making. However over the past decades untold numbers of persons have been profoundly hurt by a legalistic and negative attitude and behavior they experienced in the church, and have left by choice, or because they were rejected and told to leave. Hence any mention of a "rule" to follow and live by can evoke a huge and painful reaction. But Jesus did not call his followers – and does not call us – to follow a rule. He calls us to follow him. He says, "Come with me." It is in this coming to be with him that we discover how controlled we are by the world's rules, and how Jesus offers us a "Rhythm and Rule of Life and Prayer" that exposes and challenges the ways of the world, and leads us into life that is freeing, hospitable, kind, and life-giving in the world.

The world we live in shapes and forms us more than we ever realize. However, healthy fault lines are forming in the awareness of many persons. Questions are being asked – in the quiet of personal thought, in small group conversations, and in some recent articles and books. The longing sounds like this:
"Is this all there is?"

"Our consumer economy exists on the backs of third-world nations and their low-wage standards. Our wealth robs them of health and well-being. We need to share – water, energy, food, land, medical care."

"Protecting our western way of life becomes violent, selfish, chaotic, and tiring. The 60 hour work week is common, and many work 70 to 80 hours, just to make ends meet."

"Is there another way?"

"Numbers in attendance, meeting the budget, upkeep of the building, salaries, insurance and benefits for the ministry team and staff are what church is all about. What about reaching out? Caring for those in need and who don't feel welcome in the church? Jesus didn't build a church like this."

These thoughts – and many others – are signals of the Holy Spirit, brooding over the face of our individual and collective awareness – creating a longing for the creation of something new.

Fixing what is Broken

Along with those early followers who gathered around Jesus with their wishes and expectations, we want what is broken to be fixed. And we may well respond to Jesus' call to Come with Me with the thought that we are coming to do just that: to fix what is wrong and not working; to put the world around us back in order. But we discover that Jesus is about more than that, much more. To get in touch with that kind of "more" we need to go back to the beginning of the story to unearth what is broken, and learn how God comes to mend and heal. The story of creation (Genesis 1 and 2) reverberates with abundance, beauty, and goodness. The man and the woman God creates and places in the Garden of Eden to enjoy and to tend, find themselves surrounded by plenty – the sheer gift of God's making and giving. They see the wonder and gift in each other, and in the multitude of creatures which also inhabit this shimmering planet earth with its seas, and the skies of heaven. Created in the image and likeness of God, humankind are to tend and care for the earth and each other. God blesses them, and speaks to them of fruitfulness – not only in the trees, plants, and other created beings, but also in themselves. They also will be fruitful; they too will co-create with God. God is bringing a family of people into being.

But as the third chapter of this creation narrative opens its page, another voice enters the Garden. This voice spins a web of lies, twisting the shining vision and truth God has spoken into being. The voice asks, "Did God say, 'You shall not eat from any tree in the garden?'" The woman replies that they can eat of all the trees, except from the tree which renders the knowledge of good and evil. Taking and eating of that tree would result in death. "You shall not die," the voice declares. "God knows that when you eat of it your eyes will be opened, and you will be like God, knowing good and evil." The woman listens; she hears,

God knows their eyes will be opened. They will be like God. They will not die.

But they will have to take the fruit, and eat it. The lie penetrates her thinking, slides past God's life-giving guidance, and gives birth to the distorted desire to be wise, to be more than God had created them to be. So she takes of the fruit, gives some to her husband, and they eat.

Now what they have taken and eaten becomes a part of them--and the lie with it. Quite suddenly the world around them, their own bodies, how they see each other, how they relate to themselves – and God – changes. Naked and afraid, they hide from each other, picking leaves to make a cover. When God comes walking in the garden in the cool of the evening, they run and hide behind the trees. And when God asks "Where are you?" and "What happened?" rather than owning their choice of listening to the lie, the man blames the woman, and the woman blames the voice.

Harmony and trust are broken. The restful reality of having enough, a fruitful life together, and a deep sense of home with oneself, with each other and with God, all is shattered. The wholesome and peaceable life is fractured. All humankind has been living in this multi-fractured condition ever since: separated from one's self, from others, from creation, and from God. Death's shadow moves into the painful spaces and takes up residence there.

By the second generation of human history, one of the sons, Cain, strikes out and kills his brother, angry because of Abel's practice of worship. When God comes close, Cain refuses to own his choice to kill, but creation cries out, revealing its pain from blood spilled and buried by Cain in its soil. Afraid, Cain leaves his home, fearing that someone will now take his life; but God gives him a mark to protect him – such is the gracious tending of God in the midst of our fear and violence.

However, peace among the people, now that one person had killed another, now that the lie is in residence within and among humankind, is no more. Power and revenge reign. A page or two later in the biblical story we hear Lamech boasting to his two wives, how he has killed a man for wounding him, and a young man for striking him. And if anyone seeks revenge, they will receive death seventy-seven-fold (Genesis 4:23-24).

At our very core we are still God-created, God-breathed (Genesis 1:26,27; 2:7). God created us in love, and endowed with longing – deep at the center of our true created being—we long for God, for harmony, for connectedness with ourselves, with each other, and with creation. This side of Eden the lie has taken up residence and fabricates a split between our true self and our false, distorted self-- the self that is never at peace, never satisfied, can never have enough. The false self blames others to protect itself, and organizes all of life around itself. This is the self which traps us in our fractured condition.

God keeps coming – to heal what is broken

Only God can heal what is broken, bring life to what is dead, and mend the multi-fractured condition of our lives and world. God keeps coming. The biblical story is full of accounts of how God comes, and how people listen and respond to God, or resist and turn away. God comes to Abraham and Sarah, an elderly couple who are past the age of childbearing, and speaks words of promise and blessing – for them and for all humankind:

> Go from your country and your kindred and your father's house to the land that I will show you. I will make of you a great nation, and I will bless you, and make you a blessing . . . . in you all the families of the earth will be blessed. (Genesis 12:1-3)

Abraham and Sarah hear, and go – no map or GPS provided. Abraham is seventy-five years old as he and his servants pack up all their belongings and begin the long trek to the land God would show them. It would be another twenty-five years before the promise of a child – "I will make of you a great nation" – would come true. In the interim he worries, bargains with God that the head manager of all his affairs could become his heir. But God comes to Abraham in his sleepless nights, and invites him outside to look at the starlit sky. As Abraham lifts his head and gazes up at the stars of heaven, God again assures Abraham, "So shall your descendants be" (Genesis 15:1-6). God is helping Abraham know that God is the One who will make a great people, is the One who will bring blessing to all the families of the earth. And once more, Abraham trusts God's promise.

Sarah has her own struggle. Since God did not seem to be doing what needed to be done for the promise to come true through Sarah, like Abraham she decides that she will fix the problem. As was the custom of the culture, she gives her slave-girl Hagar to Abraham as his wife – so that Hagar could bear Abraham's child. And she does. But God does keep the promise spoken to this elderly couple. Sarah does become pregnant with Abraham's child, and she does give birth – to a baby boy. And Sarah, overcome with the joy of long-awaited life, calls out to everyone around her,

> God has brought laughter for me; everyone who hears will laugh with me . . . I have borne Abraham a son in his old age. (Genesis 21:5-7)

God is making a people – doing the impossible. God keeps coming. Through Moses, who hears God's call and leads the people of Israel out of slavery in Egypt, even as God keeps vigil and makes the great escape possible (Exodus 12:40-42). Through Judges who steer the people back to God when they wander away; through priests, and prophets, and kings, God keeps coming. But the people do not listen well – not to the laws God has given to guide them as a nation, nor to God. They turn and choose other gods to worship, and lose their way. But God still comes, speaking another promise through the prophets, the promise of a Coming One who will bring make all things new. God is about to do something new:

> I am about to do a new thing; now it springs forth, do you not perceive it? I will make a way in the wilderness and rivers in the desert . . . . To give drink to my chosen people, the people I have formed for myself so that they might declare my praise. (Isaiah 42:19-21)

God is making a people.

God comes: in Jesus

As we continue to turn the pages of the biblical narrative, we find ourselves in the New Testament (a collection of books about the new covenant, the new thing God is making). We discover that what God has promised is now coming true: Jesus is about to be born! Jesus is the One who will unroll the scroll of the prophet Isaiah and read to all gathered in the synagogue in Nazareth, why he has come:

> The Spirit of the Lord is upon me, because he has anointed me to bring good news to the poor. He has sent me to proclaim release to the captives and recovery of sight to the blind, to let the oppressed go free, to proclaim the year of the Lord's favor. (Isaiah 42:1-7; Luke 4:18-19)

Jesus comes to mend and to heal our fractured condition. As we turn to follow him, we discover what the new thing God is doing is about.

For Your Reflection

Take some time to reflect on the biblical narratives we have visited in this chapter.

What caught your attention?

When you reflect on how God comes – all through the biblical narrative – in what way are you aware of how God comes and invites your attention in your own life?

As you consider the broken condition of our world today, what do you desire?

What are your expectations as you explore a more missional and monastic way of being present in the world-as-it-is?

2
Come With Me

The Gospel Rhythm for Life and Prayer

Early in his ministry Jesus forms a rhythm in his relationship with those who follow him: coming, being with him and each other, then being sent out. We tend to focus on the being sent into all the world, but Jesus included all three movements in the life of his disciples. This rhythm becomes foundational; it is what the followers of Jesus do "as a rule" – what becomes the norm in their lives and practice. Mark's gospel invites us to join Jesus and his followers on retreat among the mountains on the north side of the Sea of Galilee:

> Jesus walks up the mountain, and calls to him those whom he wants, and they come to him. to be with him, and to be sent out. From among his followers, Jesus appoints twelve – whom he also names apostles, to be with him, to be sent out

to proclaim the message, and to have authority to cast out demons. Simon (to whom he gives the name Peter); James son of Zebedee and John the brother of James (to whom he gives the name Boanerges, that is, Sons of Thunder); and Andrew, and Philip and Bartholomew, and Matthew (the tax collector (Matthew 10:31), and Thomas, and James son of Alphaeus, and Thaddaeus, and Simon the Cananaean (who is called the Zealot Luke 6:15), and Judas Iscariot, who betrayed him.
(Mark 3:14-19, author's paraphrase)

Later Jesus will choose and appoint seventy more of his followers, to come and be with him, and then to be sent out. Jesus gives them guidance for their outward journey: they are to visit with folks in their homes, to be a presence for peace, eating at table together, receiving hospitality, tending any who are sick in the house or the surrounding town, embodying what they are announcing: "The kingdom of God has come near to you." (Luke 10:1-9)

Coming

> Jesus went up the mountain and called to him those whom he wanted, and they came to him.

We are invited into retreat – a time apart in a deserted place away from the crowd, our daily tasks, tight schedule, cell phone, texts, emails, multiple demands; all that absorbs our attention and energy and often clutters our perspective. Jesus calls us to come. Our turning aside from the daily is in response to his call. As we come we cross an initial threshold.

Being With

> They came to him . . . to be with him

This time with Jesus draws us into the place where we learn to stop and to be present. While this sounds simple, we discover that this shift to "being with" is not always easy. Even though we are in retreat on the mountainside, the agenda of the previous twenty-four hours or week continues to sound its many voices and demands within our consciousness. The act of turning off our cell phone can arouse reaction: we are more addicted to instant technology than we realize. We need to be patient. The work of the soul cannot be hurried.

Now we cross another threshold – into being more fully present. It can be helpful to name what crowds our mind, what seeks to kidnap our attention. You can either speak these things in your group, or write them down. Then offer what you have shared or written to God to keep and to tend as we are settling into this place apart.

The following prayer, which comes from the Celtic practice of retreat among the islands off the coast of Scotland and Ireland, draws us more deeply across a deeper threshold:

Hear Jesus' invitation:
>   Come to me,
>   all you that are weary
>   and are carrying heavy burdens,
>   and I will give you rest. (Matthew 11:28-10)

Pray your response:

All that I am, Lord I place in your hands;
All that I do Lord, I place in your hands;

Everything I work for, I place in your hands;
Everything I hope for, I place in your hands;

The troubles that weary me, I place in your hands;
The thoughts that disturb me, I place in your hands;
Each that I pray for, I place in your hands;
Each that I care for, I place in your hands.[6]

Enter the narrative of Mark 3:18; be present on the mountain. Be attentive. Listen.

---

[6] Northumbria Community, *Celtic Daily Prayer*. San Francisco: HarperSanFrancisco, 2002. 154-55. Taken from a Celtic prayer of Oswald of Northumbria.

Being Named: The Inward Journey

Simon . . . to whom he gave the name Peter; James son of
Zebedee and John the brother of James to whom he gave the
name Boanerges...

In this time apart Jesus will tend our inward and our outward
journey.

It was the custom in Jesus' day, to give persons nicknames – as a way
of tending their inner formation, and their life in community. This
practice is still followed in other countries of the world. Following
completion of graduate studies in Wheaton, Illinois, Joseph and his
wife, Elizabeth, and their six-year old son John, returned to their
home country in Nigeria, Africa. Elizabeth was expecting a child, and
four months later I received a letter, announcing the happy news
about the birth of their daughter. Her names? Tasi (short for
Anastasia, Greek word for the Resurrection, so that she would always
know the great hope in Jesus); Monday (because she was born on a
Monday – and would always know what day she was born on); Sleepy
(because her brother John was disappointed that Tasi slept most of
the time, and somehow he had expected that the new baby brother or
sister would be a playmate he could play with); and LeQuat (their
family, tribal name).

In the quiet of retreat Jesus gives nicknames to some of his followers:

To Simon, son of Jonas, he gives the name Peter (Petros, which
means 'rock'). Simon—as we follow his story in the gospels—reveals
that he thinks he is already a rock. But in time he learns how little he
is aware of his own weakness, and how much he avoided admitting
his fears. Jesus begins by giving him a strong name, assuring Simon
of his potential in Jesus' sight.

James and John, brothers, also need guidance for their inner journey.
Jesus gives them the name Boanerges – Sons of Thunder – thus
calling their attention to begin owning and dealing with their anger
response when confronted with certain situations. In the face of the
Samaritan villagers not granting their request for Jesus and the

disciples to have a place to stay for the night, these brothers want to command fire to come down from heaven and consume the village. Jesus calls their attention to discern the driving force behind this kind of rage that lurks within their souls.

Simon the Cananaean is invited to reflect on his beliefs and behavior as a Zealot and to get in touch with his hostile and violent reactions to persons who were not fighting for Jewish freedom from Roman Rule. This would include Levi (Matthew) whom Jesus calls away from his tax-collection booth in Capernaum, where Matthew sat day after day, working to collect taxes from Jewish citizens – tax money which paid the wages of the occupying forces of Roman soldiers and political leaders.

Sometimes the people we are called to live and work with as we follow Jesus, will arouse all kinds of negative reactions within us. As we spend time in retreat – with Jesus and each other – Jesus will continue to tend our inner journey, naming with patience and kindness those things that hold us captive, attitudes that grow out of our fractured condition, fears we may have of being known for who we truly are.

Being Named: The Outward Journey

> And he appointed twelve, whom he also named apostles, to be with him, and to be sent out to proclaim the message, and to have authority to cast out demons, and to heal.

Our gifts and strengths are named. Now we receive discernment and direction for missional ministry of companioning others into the gracious rule of God.

On the outward journey of being sent, our lives and our practice of missional life and ministry – no matter what our gift and calling – will bear the mark of Jesus' call to bring good news to the poor, confrontation of evil, release of captivity from oppression, and healing. Jesus reminds us that he goes with us, today companioned and indwelt by the Spirit of Christ who continues the work of Jesus to bring healing and wholeness to the painful fractures in which we and the world live.

For Your Reflection

Reflect on the rhythm to which Jesus calls his followers – to come, to be with him, and to respond to being sent. Then consider the following questions:

How is Jesus directing your attention to your rhythm of life, rest, prayerful solitude, and the work of ministry? In other words, how are you practicing:

Your love for your neighbor?

Notice the time you give to work, to doing, to producing
Notice the place you give to serving others, bring present to others.
In what way does your ministry flow out of your gifts?
In what way does your ministry feel tight, burdensome, tiring?

Your love for yourself?

Pay attention to the space you give to being, resting, play
Attend to the space you give to yourself, care for your self.
In what way is God inviting your attention to areas that
need attention: fear, anger, loss, disappointment, frustration?
In what way are you becoming aware of strengths, graces, gifts?

Your love for God?

Notice the space you give to God
Your awareness of God's presence across the day, the night
Your response to God
In being with God in prayerful listening
In avoidance, lack of trust, busyness
In conversation (prayer, journaling)
In action (outward response, tending, journey)

Your love for God's Good Earth?

Reflect on your awareness of creation
What do you notice that brings you joy?
What concerns you?
In what way do you appreciate and care for creation?

Take some time now to write in your journal:

a. What does your "Rule/Rhythm" of life look like? (*Love for self*)
    What is healthy and life-giving?
    What is less than life-giving, driven, compulsive?
    What is missing?
    What do you sense you need?

b. What does your "Rule of Prayer" look like? (*Love for God*)
    What do notice about your life with God?
    . . . noticing God?
    . . your response/conversation with God?
. . . your intentional practice of prayer and spiritual disciplines?

c. In what way do you gather with a community *(Love for neighbor and self in community)*
        to check in
        to listen to each other's journey and concerns individually --
                        inward
                        outward
        to discern God's presence and guidance in each other
        to discern God's presence and guidance for the community
            to pray,
            and to play?

d. In what way do you and the community you meet with enjoy and care for creation?

3
New Monastic Rule of Life

Following Jesus on a New Monastic Path

As the followers of Jesus enter into the rhythm and rule of Jesus their lives are changed. His ways become their ways. Jesus becomes their center. It is from this Center in Jesus that they live and serve. And it is to this Center that they return. Later in this workbook we will be attending to how these early followers – both the twelve and many others – return to be with Jesus and each other, in places of retreat for checking in, recounting their experience of missional ministry, for discernment, receiving spiritual guidance, prayerful tending, and blessing. United Methodists would call this a Class Meeting, or a Band Meeting, in which a question is asked:

"How is it with your soul?"

This kind of attentiveness to our inner soul and being is foreign to the world we know, and most often to the way we experience congregational life. This calls for a shift within us – even as this kind of rhythm and rule of life and missional ministry calls for a deep change within the lives of the early disciples. The "self" is now challenged to put Jesus and the new thing that God is bringing into being, in primary place. We may discover resistance within our self, and at the same time know that this is our deepest dream and desire. Conflict within our self -- and even within our missional group of journey partners -- may surface around this kind of issue. What we are experiencing is a battle going on between our false self and our deepest and true self, now being formed and transformed around Jesus.

This side of Eden, we – like Adam and Eve – tend to "hide among the trees,"[7] because we often feel fearful of God coming close. So when Jesus invites us to come, we may feel the same resistance. Simon Peter, one of the early disciples felt this same fear and resistance. He knows this same interior battle.

---

[7] See Genesis 3:8-10.

For Your Reflection

Turn to Luke's gospel, chapter 5, verses 1 – 11.
Read this narrative slowly, prayerfully, twice.
What do you notice?
What do you notice about Simon Peter?
What lies behind his rejection of Jesus?
How does Jesus respond to Simon Peter's fear?
If you were to place yourself in that boat, what would you feel as you pull up your nets, and see what is in them – in the presence of Jesus?
What would you want to say to Jesus?

Jesus calls us to lose our false self – and as we do, we find our true self. This is the way our fractured condition is healed and made whole.

Guidance from Other Pilgrims on this Missional, Monastic Path

Bishop Ken Carter of the United Methodist Church talks a bit about two ordained elders in the UMC: Elaine A. Heath, and Larry Duggins:

"In her teaching and writing, Elaine . . . has led pilgrims to thin places where the Holy Spirit pierces most, if not all, of our illusions. As denominations flatten and fragment, she and Larry . . . have become evangelists for a 'tradition behind the tradition' and strategists for a future that is missional (and) monastic . . . (a way of) healing and hope."[8]

If we have questions about what a New Monastic Rule of Life would look like today, Elaine responds by inviting us to see discipleship as a three-legged stool.[9] The flat part we sit on is doctrine – our beliefs (those things we hold as true and live into in our lives). Hence what we hold as true matters – it shapes our lives.

The three legs that support the seat are sets of practices.
One leg is a set of practices called prayer.
Another leg is a set of practices called hospitality.
The third leg is a set of practices called justice – an old-fashioned
Bible word, found plentifully in the Bible, including Micah 6:8 (CEB):
> He has told you, human one, what is good and what the Lord
> requires from you: to do justice, embrace faithful love, and
> walk humbly with your God.

The entire stool is able to support all the pieces. Disciple formation requires formation in all the practices as well as beliefs. But practices are foundational; they support the beliefs – even as they anchored in beliefs. If the word 'belief' has worn thin, and tends to fall flat in its meaning for us, Elaine calls another pilgrim to the table, Diana Butler Bass. Diana explains that the word 'belief' in Middle English really meant "be-love" – something like "love and trust."

---

[8] Heath and Duggins, *Missional. Monastic. Mainline.* See back cover.

[9] Ibid., 66 and following pages.

Elaine notes that Bass raises a wonderful question: "What would it look like if when we recited the Nicene Creed instead of saying "We believe in one God, the Father Almighty . . . we said, "We love and trust in one God, the Father Almighty?"[10] Or if we said, "We be-love one God."?

Thus, as we sit on the seat of this stool, we settle ourselves into loving trust in God.

The three legs, our practices, work together to help us learn how God relates to us, welcomes us, provides for us in peace and justice.

- prayer (the stuff of God's relationship with us and our relationship with God);
- hospitality (that open and welcoming acceptance God offers us, and that we offer others); and
- justice (seeing and responding to each other and creation through the eyes of Jesus.)

These three practices are outward signs of how we live our be-love for God, for each other, and for creation. The New Monastic Rule of Life is an expression of our be-loving and our life in action.

---

[10] Butler Bass, Diana, *Christianity After Religion: The End of the Church and the Birth of a New Spiritual Awakening.* New York: HarperOne, 2012. 128-34.

For Your Reflection

Let's pause for a moment and reflect on places in your life where rules have been less than helpful or life-giving.

Remember when rules have been helpful.

What would happen if there were no rules in place? No double-yellow lines down the center of a highway?

What do rules say about our desire for fairness, justice, reverence for life?

In what way do rules serve to shape our way of life, how we live?

As you hear the term, Rule of Life, how do you respond within yourself?

Early Monastic Rules

On one of my book shelves, standing between larger tomes of ancient Christian spiritual writings is a paper-back booklet, about 4 ¼ by 7 inches in size, small enough to be lost or overlooked. All of 96 pages in length – this little book is an English translation of *The Rule of St. Benedict*, an early monastic rule written by Benedict in the 6th Century. This Rule is still in use and has served to shape the life together and spiritual formation of many other monastic communities – also a multitude of other persons (called Benedictine Oblates) who feel the need for a way of life to sustain and guide them as they live and follow Jesus in the world-as-it-is today.

As a young adult, Benedict turned aside from his life and education in Rome, Italy, to find a place for solitude and prayerful reflection. Following the edict of Constantine in A.D. 325, all persons in the Roman Empire would now be brought into the Christian Church, a movement which inundated the churches with persons who came from a background of worshiping and serving pagan deities, thus diluting the faithful and costly commitment which Christians had lived under the threat of rejection and even arrest, imprisonment, and death for not worshiping pagan gods or the Roman emperor. Later the plundering and destruction of the Roman Empire by marauding forces from the north shattered the civil order of Roman rule. Chaos ruled. The mix of shallow Christian living and the destruction of civil order and ways of life served to pull Benedict as a young adult into seeking a Way, a Rhythm and rule of Life and Prayer that would be true to the Way of Jesus, and a Way that would be sustaining for communities of people, as well as a witness in the world.

Some monks who were seeking guidance and community approached him, and in time Benedict formed several monasteries. Together they found guidance in their life in community, guidance offered by the Rule Benedict developed. Not averse to learning, Benedict was a student of earlier works penned by other followers of Jesus, people who were seeking to learn how to live true to Jesus in a fragmented world. Benedict leaned into the writings of John Cassian,[11] who lived and wrote some 100 years earlier.[12] It is in Cassian's work that we are privy to conversations he had with more experienced monks who offered spiritual guidance. Abba Moses, considered a 'father' among the monks, explains the core intent for this monastic way of living: ". . . the end of our course is the kingdom of God." He goes on to say that for this we need "purity of heart".[13] Somehow "purity of heart" is bound up with the core intent of monastic life – seeking the Kingdom of God. Jesus also calls those who follow him to seek first the kingdom of God and God's righteousness (Matthew 6:33). We may find ourselves asking, well, just what is the Kingdom of God? And what do you mean by purity of heart, and God's righteousness?

If we reach back into the Genesis story, we find some clues as to what is being said here. When the lie was believed, and acted upon, then a deadly untruth took up residence. Death showed up in our multi-fractured condition – separation from our self, from each other, from God, and from creation. Fear ruled. This same fear gave

---

[11] Fry, Timothy, O.S.B. Ed, RB1980 *The Rule of St. Benedict in English,* The Liturgical Press, 1981. Ch.42:3 "When there are two meals, all the monks will sit together immediately after rising from supper. Someone should read from the *Conferences* . . . or at any rate something else that will benefit the hearers." 73:5 "Then, besides the *Conferences* of the Fathers, . . . there is also the rule of our holy father Basil." (The Rule of Saint Benedict is divided into 73 chapters, and each sentence or paragraph is numbered for ease of reference.)

[12] The author of the Conferences, John Cassian, along with his friend Germanus, had spent some ten years in Egypt at the turn of the 5th Century, on a pilgrimage to visit and have conversation with monks and abbas who were known for their spiritual wisdom and guidance. There, either side of the Nile River – in places of solitude and desert – lived godly men and women who, like Benedict had turned away from the chaotic and violent ways of the world, on a search for what it meant to be a true follower of Jesus. Cassian wrote what he had heard and learned as he engaged in twenty-four conversations with these desert dwellers who also lived a monastic rule of life and prayer. Cassian and Germanus were themselves monks. Cassian later became ordained to the diaconate and served the church in Constantinople; Germanus was ordained as a priest and served in Rome. Later, Cassian was also ordained as a priest and served in Rome.

[13] Abba Moses, in "First Conference: The First Conference of Abba Moses: On the Goal and the End of the Monk." I.IV.1. 42-3

birth to the belief that one's identity would depend on what could be accumulated (Do I have enough?), or what one produced (Did I make enough?) No longer is our life and identity recognized as God-created and God-given gifts. We need to work to make ourselves somebody. Or as we tend to say in our western world, "Life only happens if we make it happen." The inner source of our life became contaminated. The well-spring of our soul became muddied.[14] When Jesus says, "Blessed are the pure in heart, for they will see God," he is calling our attention to how muddied the source of our life is this side of Eden. We need something to un-muddy the source. This is not something we can do ourselves – no matter how many rules we obey, and regulations we follow. Only God, the divine physician, can heal what is fractured, mend what is broken. Only God can tend the very source of our being, and un-muddy the source. Hence the psalmist prays: "Create in me a clean heart, O God, and renew a right spirit within me" (Psalm 51:10).

This is how God comes – to mend and to heal. Jesus says, "I have not come to call the righteous but sinners" (Matthew 9:13). So, as we follow Jesus around in the gospels, and in life today, we begin to live in to the Kingdom of God, and we discover that the very source of our life and being is gradually being un-muddied. Hence the call to listen: Pay attention to how you listen. The lie of Eden has spawned a million other untruths which riddle into the world's way of living. We are called to listen to God, to Jesus. As we listen and lean into God's ways, the gracious path of Jesus, we are changed. Hence Benedict begins writing The Rule as way of guiding the life, prayer, work, and mission of the community by saying,

> Listen carefully . . . with the ear of your heart.
> Benedict (Rule. Prologue, 1)

A monastic community is designed, therefore, to offer guidance for the community of Christian believers who walk the way of Jesus towards this goal. In this we find the desire to live into the kingdom of God, even as we are living within the "kingdom" of this world.

---

[14] Tugwell, Simon. *The Beatitudes: Soundings in the Christian Tradition.* Templegate Publishers, 1980. 94-95.

Hence, in our search today for a way to live and be in the world-as-it-is, in the face of the church-as-it-is, we find companions in our ancient past, pilgrims and seekers who found they needed a Rule to guide them. The monastic way becomes a school of conversion and transformation.

Discovering a Guide – A Rule – For Today

Here we listen to other pilgrims – persons in the United Methodist Church who offer us guidance for a new monastic rule today. "The most obvious place for Methodists to begin thinking about a rule is with a reading of Wesley's General Rules for Methodist Societies. (found in the United Methodist Church Book of Discipline). These are organized into three categories (Elaine's paraphrase):

1.   First, do no harm.
2.   Do all the good you can.
3.   Practice individual and corporate spiritual disciplines.

As did St. Benedict with his three-fold rule (conversion, obedience, and stability), underneath each precept Wesley detailed a variety of applications, such as refusing to own slaves, and practicing frugality.

"It is striking to see how many of Wesley's applications are consistent with the twelve marks of the new monasticism.[15] Another alternative that could be helpful to the whole church, would be for the rule to follow the fivefold structure of membership vows in the United Methodist Church (see United Methodist Book of Discipline, 103). When joining the United Methodist Church, candidates vow to 'be loyal to the United Methodist Church and uphold it with their prayers, presence, gifts, service, and witness.' "[16]

---

[15] Rutba House, *Schools for Conversion: Twelve Marks of a New Monasticism.* Cascade Publishers.

[16] Heath and Kisker, *Longing.* 51.

These five membership vows can become a supportive structure "that helps us learn the essential practices together with their theological foundations. . . . By following a rule of life together, and having covenant accountability in small groups for how we are following it, we have ongoing opportunities to build a strong, solid three-legged stool of discipleship."[17]

The following is the Rule of Life that the Missional Wisdom Foundation and its various ministries has developed over time, and which offers the kind of structure and guidance that we need in our various communities as we seek to be faithful disciples of Jesus – in what we believe (be-love), and in our practices of prayer, hospitality, and justice.

Across our pilgrimage together, into the gospel narratives, and on this missional journey, we will be living into this New Monastic Rule of Life. In our practice we will become aware of how the five-fold rule within the United Methodist tradition becomes a living expression of the way of Jesus. It is not the rule itself to which we are bound, but to Jesus Christ whom we love and serve, and who now lives within us through the Holy Spirit, and who empowers and transforms us as we co-labor with God in the world. The following sections in the guide will offer guidance for our daily living of the Rule.

---

[17] Heath, Elaine A., and Larry Duggins, *Missional. Monastic. Mainline. A Guide to Starting Missional Micro-Communities in Historically Mainline Traditions.* Cascade Books, 2014. 68.

A NEW MONASTIC RULE OF LIFE

Prayers
- We will pray daily
- We will use a variety of forms of prayer such as the reflective reading of Scripture and other spiritual texts, confession, the prayer of examen, intercession, journaling, and contemplation
- We will regularly fast

Presence
- We will practice a contemplative stance in order to be present to God, the world, and ourselves
- We will be hospitable to our neighbors in our families, neighborhoods, and workplaces
- We will be hospitable to our faith community through participation in our worship, fellowship and mission

Gifts
- We will honor and care for the gift of the earth and its resources, practicing ecologically responsible living, striving for simplicity rather than excessive consumption
- We will practice generosity in sharing our material resources, including money, within and beyond this community
- We will use our spiritual gifts, talents and abilities to serve God within and beyond this community

Service
- We will serve God and neighbor out of gratitude for the love of God
- We will practice mutual accountability with a covenant group within the community, for how we serve God and neighbor
- We will practice regular Sabbath as a means of renewal so that we can lovingly serve God and neighbor

Witness
- We will practice racial and gender reconciliation
- We will resist evil and injustice
- We will pursue peace with justice
- We will share the redeeming, healing, creative love of God in word, deed and presence in order to invite others to Christian discipleship.

4
Living the New Monastic Rule: Prayer

We will pray daily

We will use a variety of forms of prayer such as the reflective
reading of Scripture and other spiritual texts, confession, the prayer
of examen, intercession, journaling, and contemplation

We will regularly fast

Coming

Jesus went up the mountain and called to him those whom he wanted

> ... And they came to him ... to be with him.
> (Mark 3:13)

The spiritual discipline here is for us to hear Jesus' call: 'Come with me,"
> to turn aside from our every-day work, and
> to come to be with him, to be with God.

We tend to think that we take the initiative when it comes to prayer, that we begin the conversation with God. But in reality, we turn to God in prayer because the Spirit of God is tugging at our attention, awakening in us the desire to come to God in prayer. Our practice of prayer is primary, and takes precedence. Without prayer our practice of discipleship becomes self-directed, off-balance, a two-legged stool.

Finding a Place

While it is true that we can pray anywhere, and at any time – God is present everywhere and at all times – as we begin this "Come with me" pilgrimage with Jesus, we discover that Jesus chooses places of solitude and quiet for prayer. His early followers find that difficult to understand, but learn to go with him:

In the morning, while it was still very dark, he got up and went out to a deserted place, and there he prayed. And Simon and his companions hunted for him. When they found him, they said to him, "Everyone is searching for you."

He answered, "Let us go on to the neighboring towns, so that I may proclaim the message there also; for that is what I came out to do." (Mark 1:32-38)

Time apart in a place of solitude for prayer and listening to God, frees us from the clamor and drivenness of many demands, offers rest for our own care, and guidance for ministry.

Whenever you pray go to your room, shut the door
and pray to your Father who is in secret; and your Father who sees in
secret will reward you. (Matthew 6:6)

When we do feel that nudging to stop, to turn aside from the daily,
and to come apart for prayer, where do we go? If you have moved
house recently you may well feel dislocated. A change of job, or some
other change in our lives can also disturb our daily routine and
rhythm. During times like these we tend to "lose our place" and may
experience difficulty in returning to a regular rhythm and place for
prayer.

Other pilgrims also experienced similar changes, and discovered ways
to create places and to be with God.

From there Abram moved on to the hill country on the east of
Bethel, and pitched his tent . . .
And there he built an altar to the LORD and invoked the name of
the LORD. (Genesis 12: 8,9)

Places can have special meaning for us, and can help evoke our
attention and presence for God – who is always present to us.

Abram and Nathanael found a shady tree to sit under
(Genesis 18:1; John 1:45-49)

Jacob chose a stone as a reminder of God's
presence and as a place to pray
(Genesis 28:11-18)

Hagar prayed by a well of water
(Genesis 16:7-14)

Simon Peter went up on a roof-top to pray at noon
(Acts 10:9)

Each of these pilgrims discovered a place - where they drew aside to
be with God. And each one found something to assist them in their
presence with God.

For Your Reflection

Reflect on those times and places in your life
where you felt close to God.

Where were some of those "God places" for you?

Tending The Space

> Abram moved on the hill country on the
> east of Bethel, and pitched his tent,
> with Bethel on the west and Ai on the east;
> and there he built an altar to the LORD
> and invoked the name of the LORD.
> (Genesis 12:8)

As you walk through your home, or through the church building – or maybe another space – what "place" invites your soul to stay, to be with God in that sacred place?

What do you need as you seek to create and tend this sacred place?

Possibly one or more of the following:

a bible
a candle and candle holder
a favorite stone
a shell
an empty dish, or maybe a dish filled with water
a wood carving
a small water fountain
a plant
a journal, and a favorite pen or pencil to write with
a favorite chair; a kneeling bench; a pillow
a CD player or mp3 player

Remember, less is always more.

Settling Into a Rhythm: Times for Prayer

+ WE WILL PRAY DAILY +

I call upon God,
and the Lord will save me.
Evening and morning and at noon . . .
he will hear my voice.
(Psalm 55:16,17)

Prayer is like food and water: prayer sustains the soul in the same way that food and water sustain our body. Prayer is like breathing: breath sustains our life across the day and the night. We cannot live without prayer.

The early church followed the Hebrew rhythm of times for prayer.

O LORD, in the morning you hear my voice (Psalm 5:3)

By day the LORD commands his steadfast love, and at night his song is with me, a prayer to the God of my life. (Psalm 42:8)

It is good to give thanks to the LORD,
to sing praises to your name, O Most High;
to declare your steadfast love in the morning
and your faithfulness by night. (Psalm 92:1,2)

One day Peter and John were going up to the temple at the hour of prayer at three o'clock in the afternoon. (Acts 3:1)

In the Book of Common Prayer – a prayer book designed to sustain and guide God's people in their prayer and in their worship, there is a section, "Daily Devotions for Individuals and Families." Grounded in the monastic rhythm of the Benedictine order, guidance is offered for prayer across the span of the day:

> In the Morning
> At Noon
> In the Early Evening
> At the Close of the Day[18]

The pace of our western world, the pressures of work and ministry, the insistence of demands and expectations of others, hold us captive and override our desire to stop, to come to a place apart, and to be with God.   But it is in this place and in these times with God that we are freed from the tyranny of these demands and the many "voices" which demand our attention and obedience.

> In the morning while it was still very dark,
> he got up and went out to a deserted place,
> and there he prayed.
> And Simon and his companions hunted for him.
> When the found him, they said to him,
> "Everyone is searching for you."
>
> He answered,
> "Let us go on to the neighboring towns,
> so that I may proclaim the message there also;
> for that is what I came out to do."
> (Mark 1:35 – 38)

---

[18] Oxford University Press, 1990. Pp.136 -140.

For Your Reflection

In Chapter One you took some time to reflect on your own rhythm and rule of life and prayer. Look it over, and then consider what changes you desire to make, especially in light of choosing time (times) for prayer?

What might your emerging rhythm of life and prayer look like?

Being With: Speaking and Listening in Prayer

As you continue on this pilgrimage – for spiritual formation and for missional engagement – you will be receiving guidance for your practice of each of the forms of prayer included in the rule. In this chapter we will enter into the practice of Reflective Reading of Scripture. This spiritual discipline has been practiced by other pilgrims of faith for centuries. As we leaf through the prayers of the book of psalms, we come across a prayer asking God to give understanding:

> Make me understand the way of your precepts,
> And I will meditate on your wondrous works . . . .
> I ruin the way of your commandments,
> For you enlarge my understanding . . . .
> The unfolding of your words gives light;
> It imparts understanding to the simple.
> (Psalm 119:27, 32, 130)

What we are hearing, is that as the person praying speaks the words with the mouth, and repeats the words in their mind, the meaning of what is read/spoken sinks to a deeper level, bringing understanding and light for what is obscure and unknown. Jesus, in reflecting on this deep, receptive listening, says that this soul understanding then leads to a turning to God that brings healing to all of life (Matthew 13:14-15). Thus, this spiritual discipline cooperates with God's desire and our need – for inner healing from our fractured condition. Practiced across the centuries, this prayer practice—also named Lectio Divina (Sacred Reading)--became a foundational spiritual discipline among the Benedictine monastic communities.

Other prayer forms --confession, the prayer of examen, intercession, journaling, contemplation, fasting – we will be learning and practicing as we focus on each of the other practices of the Rule: Presence, Gifts, Service and Witness.

+ WE WILL USE A VARIETY OF FORMS OF PRAYER +

Reflective Reading of Scripture (and other Spiritual Texts)[19]

We tend to approach prayer as speaking to God, praying prayers to God. And often we find ourselves thinking more about what we are saying in prayer than who we are praying to. Prayer can often become a one-way street. However, prayer in the biblical narrative is a conversation. The prophet Isaiah writes:

> The Lord God has given me the tongue of one who is taught, that I may know how to sustain the weary with a word. Morning by morning [God] wakens – wakens my ear. To listen as those who are taught. The Lord God has opened my ear.
> (Isaiah 50:4-5)

Jesus also says:

> Pay attention to how you listen. (Luke 8:16)

A spiritual discipline which leads us into this kind of receptive, listening, and contemplative prayer is Lectio Divina or "sacred reading." To begin with, allow 20 minutes for this prayer practice, and a few minutes for engaging in the 'For Your Reflection' questions, either as you pray individually, or with a covenant group. The five movements of Lectio Divina include:

> Prayer for openness
> Read
> Meditate
> Respond to God in prayer
> Be still

You may use this receptive and reflective prayer practice with various passages of scripture, or spiritual writings.

---

[19] Biblical and historical background for content and guidance for the practice of Lectio Divina is given in Miller, Wendy. *Invitation to Presence: A Guide to Spiritual Disciplines.* Upper Room Books, 1995. Pp. 44-59.

+ LECTIO DIVINA:
RECEPTIVE READING OF SCRIPTURE   +

Lectio divina (Sacred Reading) is a spiritual discipline which helps us to come to the scriptures as a listener, receptive to being formed into the image of Jesus Christ. This receptive and meditative reading allows the scripture to enter deeply into our thinking, and into our soul. Here the scripture begins to read our life, to bring light and guidance to our spiritual journey, and inner formation by the Holy Spirit. This prayer form is an antidote to the "reading-to-accumulate-information" and "master-the-text" method which is entrenched within our western world. Meditation on scripture was a spiritual discipline practiced by the people of God in the scriptures, and became a "throughout-the-day" spiritual discipline within the Benedictine Order founded in the 6th Century. It continues to be practiced by God's people today.

> Make me understand the way of your precepts, and I will meditate on your wondrous works . . . .
>
> I run the way of your commandments, for you enlarge my understanding . . . the unfolding of your words gives light; it imparts understanding to the simple.   (Psalm 119:27, 32, 130)

a. *Prayer for Openness*

After an initial prayer for openness to God "who is at work in you" (Phil. 2:13), read the text twice, slowly.

> Very truly, I tell you, . . . the one who enters by the gate is the shepherd of the sheep. The gatekeeper opens the gate for him, and the sheep hear his voice. He calls his own sheep by name and leads them out. When he has brought out all his own, he goes ahead of them, and the sheep follow him because they know his voice. They will not follow a stranger...
>
> I am the good shepherd. I know my own and my own know me, just as the Father knows me and I know the Father. And

I lay down my life for the sheep. My sheep hear my voice. I know them, and they follow me. I give them eternal life, and they will never perish. No one will snatch them out of my hand.
(John 10:1-4, 14-15, 27-28)

b. Read

As you read the second time, pause when a word or phrase stands out for you. This may not be a strong awareness, but when your attention is drawn to, or slowed down by a word or phrase, stay with that word or phrase. You do not need to read further in the passage.

c. Meditate on the word or phrase.

Allow it to sound slowly in your thinking. Reflect on its meaning. Allow the word or phrase to sink gradually to deeper levels of your understanding and inner awareness.

d. Respond to God in prayer about what you are discovering as God uses the word from scripture to read and to enter your life.

e. Be still.
Simply rest in the spacious and gracious presence of God.

For Your Reflection

What word or phrase invited your attention?

As you stayed with that word or phrase, what did you notice "unfolding" for you? In what way did this "unfolding" begin to "read" your life – visit various places in your life?

Was there anything that seemed to kidnap your attention away from this prayerful meditation?

What helped you return and re-focus?

What do you sense God's invitation may be to you?

For your inward journey?

For your outward journey?

Across the Week

Take the word or phrase with you, and continue to repeat it to yourself, to "pray this scripture" across the day, the night, the week. Allow God to continue speaking to you as this piece of scripture works its way more deeply into your soul, your inner being – and sheds light on your life with God, with others, with self, and with creation.

Continue to make a note in your journal of your experience.

For Your Small Group or Community Reflection[20]

When you meet and share with each other your experience of living the Rule, some questions to include are:

In what way(s) did you experience prayer over this this last week? Since we last met?

In what ways do you fast? Remember, fasting is not always from food.

In what ways do you need support or guidance in the development of your practice of prayer and fasting?

(Entries from "For Your Reflection" as you practice this spiritual discipline of Lectio Divina can be helpful as you share your experience of prayer with each other.)

---

[20] See Heath and Duggins, *Missional. Monastic. Mainline*, pp. 84-85 for some ideas for the content and rhythm of your group meetings.

5
Living the New Monastic Rule: Presence

We will practice a contemplative stance in order to be
present to the world and ourselves.

We will be hospitable to our neighbors
in our families, neighborhoods, workplaces.

+ WE WILL PRACTICE A CONTEMPLATIVE STANCE IN ORDER TO BE PRESENT TO THE WORLD AND OURSELVES. +

Being fully present calls for us to recognize and lay aside the inner "noise" and "clutter" which kidnaps us, and holds us hostage. We are more addicted to cell phones and other electronic devices than we like to admit. We tend to find our identity in what we own – house, cars, clothes, many things, or what we can produce. Tilden Edwards, Episcopal priest and founder of the Shalem Institute for Spiritual Formation, observes that we have a tendency to turn all of our time into work time.

A major reason for this is a view of reality that is reinforced by so many social forces today: a view that sees the basic reality and purpose of life as the cultivation of a separate ego needing to fulfill itself through the accumulation of many things, material and immaterial. . . . This drivenness is deepened by what sociologists call the rapid shift from ascribed to achieved status in modern societies: the shift from sensing a givenness to who we are through family, religion, and community membership, to defining ourselves (and being defined by others) in terms of what we produce through whatever individual way of life this production of self and things may involve. Today we could also include what we consume as part of our identity: our consumption of education, material goods, public events, mass media, etc. Such consumptive activity can involve as much drivenness as our productivity.[21]

This kind of drivenness kidnaps our attention so that we try to make something happen. We find ourselves driven to either produce or consume. We culturally conditioned for this reaction.

While hiking on a trail in a national park in Virginia, my husband Ed and I were surprised as the forest trail we were walking led us out to an opening which offered a stunning overlook of the Blue Ridge Mountains. We stood, silent, transfixed, and full of wonder as we gazed at the many-layered gray-blue landscape spread out before us.

---

[21] Edwards, Tilden. *Sabbath Time.* Upper Room Books, 2003. Pp. 16.

After a few minutes, two children ran out of the forest and then came and stood beside us. About ten or eleven, the boy and the girl did not speak. They simply stood rapt in wonder, in contemplation. Then a man and a woman emerged from the forest, and stood at its edge. They yelled, "Come on, you two! Let's go!." But the boy and girl stood, and said, "Oh, but you have to see this! Come and see!." And then the parents replied, "There's nothing there! Get going." "Mom and Dad, you've got to see this," the boy said. "It's so beautiful," added his sister. But the parents stayed at the forest edge, and yelled again, "We're leaving. Get going! There's nothing there to see. We've got a hike to do!" With a sigh, the two children turned and left.

In their busy, goal-driven existence, these parents had forgotten what it is like to see, to gaze, to be fully present. Teresa of Avila, abbess of a number of Carmelite community houses in the 16th century Spain, writes, "There are many ways of being in a place."[22] She is speaking to how our attention wanders, how we fail to be fully present, even as our bodies are somewhere else. Being contemplative is a way of being present, being receptive and attentive to where we are, what is before us, who we are with, as well as being present to our selves.

The spiritual disciplines of silence, the consciousness examen, and entering the narrative of scripture become helpful here. They help us become open to God's tending and re-ordering of our inner space, dealing with the kind of clutter and pre-occupation with things that block our being hospitable and receptive. Gradually we learn to be contemplatively present, to become awake to how we see and relate to God, to others, to creation, and to ourselves.

In 1145 AD a monk in the Clairvaux monastery where Bernard served as abbot, was elected to become Pope. The rhythm and rule of life and prayer of this monk-become-Pope Eugenius III is no longer guided by the Cistercian monastery where he practiced the seven monastic hours across the day and the night, each one drawing him into prayerful presence and mindfulness of God. Caught up in the

---

[22] Teresa of Avila, *Interior Castle*, Translated and Edited by E. Allison Peers, (New York: Image, 1989), 31.

multitude of papal responsibilities, he finds no time for prayer and contemplation.

Bernard is aware of how this new life and work as Pope pulls this former monk into an active life which allows little or no time for him to be mindful of his own humanity, and his own self in the presence of God. Serving as his spiritual director, Bernard writes him a series of letters which finally become five short books entitled, On Consideration. Bernard counsels Pope Eugenius to be present to himself as a man, and not to be caught up in the papal pressures of daily business.

He writes:
If you wish to belong altogether to other people, like him who was made all things to all men, I praise your humanity, but only on condition that it be complete. But how can it be complete if you yourself are left out? You, too, are a man. So then, in order that your humanity may be entire and complete, let your bosom, which receives all, find room for yourself also. . . . In short if a man is bad to himself, to whom is he good? . . . (S)et aside some portion of your heart and of your time for consideration . . .
What is so essential to the worship of God is the practice to which [God] exhorts in the Psalm, 'Be still and know that I am God.' This certainly is the chief object of consideration.

At the heart of Bernard's concern was what was "most essential in any spirituality: the difficulty of remaining centered in God while greatly involved in the service of one's neighbor."[23]

If we are to love God, and to love our neighbor as we love our self, we do need to make room for our self. Only then does our neighbor take his and her rightful place in our lives, along with our hospitable work of monastic and missional engagement.

---

[23] Anderson, John D. and Elizabeth T. Kennan, Trans. *Five Books on Consideration: Advice to a Pope. The Works of Bernard of Clairevaux,* Vol. 13. Kalamazoo, MI: Cistercian Publications, 1976. Pp. 33, 37.

The practice of the various movements of the New Monastic Rule helps us to stand back from a life of action, and to become aware of our own self-care and of God who invites us come and rest, and be restored (Psalm 23; Matthew 11:28- 30). Gradually we learn to be present to ourselves and present to God. Out of this contemplative presence we can then be fully present to our neighbor, and to creation.

For Your Reflection

In what way does your practice of your rhythm and rule offer space for leisure and care for your self? Love of your self?

Space for love of God?

What do you need?

What do you really need?

What is your deepest need?

+ WE WILL BE HOSPITABLE TO OUR NEIGHBORS: IN OUR FAMILIES +

Our spouse and our children are our closest neighbors. While we are learning to "cross the street" in order to be present to the "man" or "woman" who is needy and suffering at the side of the road, we can sometimes forget that our immediate family is also our neighbor.

Roger was serving in a two-point charge and attending seminary. The two small congregations understood his need for time for seminary studies, and respected that Roger was married and had two sons, one six and the other ten. But the newness of being licensed and installed in ministry felt like a tsunami. Swamped with concerns about keeping up with all the responsibilities, preparing sermons, attending committee meetings, completing academic readings, and writing papers, Roger began to lose sight of his family. Like the congregation, his family should understand that he was now in seminary, and in congregational ministry. However, in his second semester of the first year, he was required to take a formation course in which he was introduced to spiritual disciplines.

One of the disciplines was to pay attention to his rhythm and rule of life and prayer. Roger came to the assignment as if it were an academic seminary paper, but soon discovered that this was not what was being asked. Rather he was being asked to spend time in prayerful consideration about love for his neighbor – his closest neighbor. He couldn't even remember the last time he had been truly present to his children – or his wife, Connie.

He sat at his desk and stared out of the window, feeling numb, distant, and suddenly tired. If it had been late evening, he would have turned on the TV and watched whatever show was on that night. He had fallen into that habit – a kind of numbing for his anxiety, and an escape from the load of ministry and studies. But in that gray, empty space of presence this afternoon, he gradually became conscious of voices – the voices of his two sons, Ben and Jon, as they tried to shoot baskets into the old hoop attached to the garage in the driveway below. And then Connie's laughter as she stepped out of the side door and took a picture of them playing together.

Roger knew what he needed to write as he considered his own rhythm and rule of life and prayer. As an act of love for himself, he needed space to be, simply be, and to listen: to God, to the sounds around him, And he needed to play, to give time and presence to his children, and to Connie – his closest neighbors. That belonged in his rule of life.

Feeling lighter, he ran down the stairs and joined Ben and Jon, shooting baskets, listening to their banter, and entering into their world. Connie took another photo: "I love you, Rog," she said. "And you, Ben, and you, Jon."

For Your Reflection

In what way are you present to your family?

Your spouse?

Your children? Sons, Daughters?

Your family of origin? Father, Mother, Brothers, Sisters?

Your wider family? Uncles, Aunts, Cousins, Grandparents?

In what way are you absent, not listening, not noticing?

+ WE WILL BE HOSPITABLE TO OUR NEIGHBORS: IN OUR NEIGHBORHOODS +

Taking a prayerful walk around and through our neighborhood brings us into physical contact with the sidewalk, the street, the buildings, the houses, and the people who live, play, and work there.

Clayt Keupfer was asked to be interim pastor in a new church planting located in the northeast quadrant of Harrisonburg, Virginia. This part of the city was known for its cultural mix, also for drug trafficking, trouble, and families in need. After arriving at the church building on Kelly Street, Clayt wondered how he should begin this interim ministry. In seminary he had learned to be still and listen for God. He had also learned to be still and to contemplate what was before him: people, the city, and now – this neighborhood.

As he waited in stillness, day after day, one of his breath prayers became: "God, how are you wanting to work in this place?"

Clayt began walking the neighborhood, slowly, prayerfully. He paid attention to the children playing in front of some of the houses. He noticed some vacant lots. He got in touch with the mix of cultures: African American, Hispanic, White, Asian. He began to learn some of the neighborhood stories – of couples who were hardworking and who dreamed of buying a house, but who did not know how they could afford one. He became aware of persons who were disabled, and mentally challenged; of youth who hung around the neighborhood, and of where the hot drug spots were. Also of how the police patrolled the area – in vehicles, on bikes, and on foot.

Clayt had worked in housing construction before attending seminary, and as he continued to wait, to walk and to pray, he became aware of a vision emerging within his mind and soul: What about something like Habitat for Humanity, but a mission more locally and congregationally focused? A vision of a group of volunteers who would be able to build houses, helping single parents and couples find ways to manage their money so that they could buy a home – that they could also help build. And then as these volunteers would be at work, they could also be present to the children in the neighborhood, and the youth. A neighborhood conversation could also be happening, even as they worked to build houses.

He finally began to share this vision with the congregational leadership, and with some other persons in neighborhood churches. HOPE builders was born. It became a missional presence and ministry in that "Calcutta" section of Harrisonburg. Years later, after Clayt had graduated from seminary and responded to a call to minister in an inner city mix of apartment dwellers in Toronto, Ontario, HOPE builders is still a missional and communal presence. Families have been strengthened, children feel safe on the streets, and empty abandoned lots have become houses of welcome and hospitality in the neighborhood.

For Your Reflection

Who lives in your neighborhood?

Where are natural gathering places for people in your neighborhood?

What are some first steps you might take to become more familiar with the people and their stories in your neighborhood?

+ HOSPITALITY THROUGH PARTICIPATION IN WORSHIP AND TENDING WORSHIP AS A SPIRITUALLY FORMATIVE PRACTICE +

As with prayer, in worship we also cross various thresholds into deeper and more receptive presence – for God, for our self, and for others. In our practice of worship – whether it is in the sanctuary of the church building, in the living room of a community house, in an apartment building where a missional church gathers, or a store front gathering, our intent is always the same. We are the people of God, coming into the presence of God. Psalm 95 helps us to tend this physical and spiritual action of coming, of crossing thresholds into worship and the restorative and re-creative presence of God as we worship together.

Reflecting on Worship Through the Lens of Psalm 95

First threshold:
Worship as gathering to enter into God's presence:

> Psalm 95:1-3
> O come, let us sing to the LORD;
> Let us make a joyful noise to the rock of our salvation. Let us come into his presence with thanksgiving; . . .

Second threshold:
Worship as entering into the reality of God's Great Story – crossing the threshold from the world's distorted belief regarding power and control, to the freeing awareness of God Who holds and sustains all of creation – creation which God made and gives us as a gift to enjoy.

> Psalm 95:4-5
> For the LORD is a great God,
> And a great King above all gods.
> In his hand are the depths of the earth;
> The heights of the mountains also.
> The sea is his, for he made it,
> And the dry land, which his hands have formed.

Third threshold:

Worship as being in the field of the God who is Good Shepherd, and being restored there – being re-oriented to who we truly are – crossing the threshold into deeper presence, being with God, resting in God's presence.

> Psalm 95:6-7
> O come, let us worship and bow down,
> Let us kneel before the LORD our Maker!
> For he is our God,
> And we are the people of his pasture,
> And the sheep of his hand.

Fourth threshold:

Worship as listening to God's voice:
Familiarizing ourselves with God's voice – in contrast to many other voices.

> Psalm 95:7b
> O that today you would listen to his voice!

Fifth threshold:

We go forth into the world as God's people. The world where many voices demand our attention and loyalty: "Buy this! "Be thin!" "Be rich!" "What's in your wallet?"

We tend to forget who we are, and who God is. And so the psalmist calls us to remember a wilderness story, when the children of Israel--God's people--forgot who they were, and denied God's presence.

> Psalm 95:8-11
> Do not harden your hearts, as at Meribah,
> as on that day in the wilderness, when your ancestors tested me, and put me to the proof, though they had seen my work.
> . . These are a people whose hearts go astray, and they do not regard my ways . . . They shall not enter my rest.
> (See Exodus 17:1-7)

Voices of the world, and our false self, both negate God by speaking and acting as if God were not present, and does not count. A functional atheism emerges. (This section of the psalm refers to the wilderness narrative in Exodus 17, when the children of Israel did not believe that God was with or among them – in spite of the presence of the pillar of fire a night, and the cloud by day. And in spite of the great escape from slavery God had done on their behalf.) This is not the way of peace, of resting in God's presence, care and guidance.

Reflecting on Hospitality Within the Flow of Worship

In what way does our worship together pay attention to the various thresholds, ushering those who worship into deeper presence?

Threshold of gathering

Threshold of entering into the reality of God's Great Story

Threshold of entering in the field of the Shepherding God

Threshold of listening for God's voice

Threshold of returning into the world – to love and serve the Lord

+ HOSPITALITY THROUGH PARTICIPATION IN FELLOWSHIP +

Some weeks after the "quiet Pentecost"[24] of the upper room on the evening of that first resurrection Sunday (John 20:19-23), the fuller coming of the Holy Spirit sweeps into the lives of all of those who have come to know and follow Jesus (Acts 2). When the day of Pentecost comes, they are all together in one place.

Suddenly from heaven there came a sound like the rush of a violent wind, it filled the entire house where they were sitting. Divided tongues, as of fire, appeared among them, and a tongue rested on each of them. All of them were filled with the Holy Spirit and began to speak in other languages, as the Spirit gave them ability (1-4).

Awe came upon everyone, because many wonders and signs were being done by the apostles. All who believed were together and had all things in common; they would sell their possessions and goods and distribute the proceeds to all, as any had need. Day by day they spent much time together in the temple, they broke bread at home and ate their food with glad and generous hearts, praising God and having the good will of all the people. And day by day the Lord added to their number those who were being saved (42-47).

---

[24] The term "Quiet Pentecost" comes from the title of Dr. Dwight H. Judy's book, *Quiet Pentecost: Inviting the Spirit into Congregational Life*, Upper Room Books, 2013. Dr. Judy notes that "Over the past thirty years, a quiet revolution has been occurring in Christian life. . . . People are being touched in surprising ways by experiences with Jesus . . . inspired to live more faithfully in the challenge to love God with all of our heart and soul and mind and strength and our neighbor as ourselves" (Judy, 1-2). A sustaining image for Judy in his work is "the distinction in the New Testament between the resurrection appearances of Jesus and the moment of Pentecost reported in the book of Acts."

For Your Reflection

We are invited into this early church narrative.

As we walk among these many believers, sit with them at table, accompany them to the temple at the times for prayer, we may also find our hearts moved to begin opening our wallets, or giving away possessions to meet the needs of others within this new community. As we break bread together in their homes, learn, walk, pray, give, listen, worship together, we learn a new way, a new rule of life in community in the body of Christ.

This is participating in the fellowship – and being transformed as we do.

As you walk into the Acts narrative, and find yourself present with these early believers, what catches your attention?

In what way are you nurturing time and space for fellowship? Participating in fellowship?

+ HOSPITALITY TO OUR FAITH COMMUNITY THROUGH PARTICIPATION IN MISSION +

Missional Hospitality

Within the scriptures we discover the Great Story of God – contained in the biblical narratives – each offering us a window into the Great Story. Within this Great Story of God our own restricted and distorted story is also contained, the story of how life is for us this side of Eden. God enters into our "after Eden" space, inviting us to recognize where and who we are. God rekindles within us the desire to live into the Great Story of God, rather than being held captive by the distorted story of this world. Gradually as we live into the divine story we begin to see more clearly how constricted, fearful, selfish and violent our world is.

Seeing as Jesus Sees

In the gospel narratives we find Jesus calling his followers to pay attention to how they see:

Matthew 9:35-38 How Jesus sees the multitudes:

> Then Jesus went about all the cities and villages, teaching in their synagogues, and proclaiming the good news of the kingdom, and curing every disease and sickness.

> When he saw the crowds, he had compassion on them, because they were harassed and helpless, like sheep without a shepherd. Then he said to his disciples, "The harvest is plentiful, but the laborers are few; therefore ask the Lord of the harvest to send out laborers into his harvest."

Luke 7:36-50 How Jesus sees a woman in the city, who was a sinner:

> One of the Pharisees asked Jesus to eat with him, and he went into the Pharisee's house and took his place at the table. And a woman in the city, who was a sinner, having learned that he was eating in the Pharisee's house, brought an

alabaster jar of ointment. She stood behind him at his feet, weeping, and began to bath his feet with her tears and to dry them with her hair. Then she continued kissing his feet and anointing them with the ointment.

Now when the Pharisee who had invited him saw it, he said to himself, "If this man were a prophet he would have known who and what kind of woman this is who is touching him – that she is a sinner." . . . The turning toward the woman, Jesus said to Simon, "Do you see this woman? I entered your house; you gave me no water for my feet, but she has bathed my feet with her tears and dried them with her hair. You gave me no kiss, but from the time I came in she has not stopped kissing my feet. You did not anoint my head with oil, but she has anointed my feet with ointment. Therefore I tell you, her sins, which were many, have been forgiven;" . . . The he said to her, "Your sins are forgiven."

But those who were at the table with him began to say among themselves, "Who is this who even forgives sins?" And he said to the woman, "Your faith has saved you; go in peace."

Luke 7:11-16 How Jesus sees a grieving widow:

Jesus went to a town called Nain, and his disciples and a large crowd went with him. As he approached the gate of the town, a man who had died was being carried out. He was his mother's only son, and she was a widow; and with her was a large crowd from the town. When the Lord saw her he had compassion for her and said to her, "Do not weep." Then he came forward and touched the bier, and the bearers stood still. And he said, "Young man, I say to you, rise!" The dead man sat up and began to speak, and Jesus gave him to his mother.

Fear seized all of them; and they glorified God, saying, "A great prophet has risen among us!" and "God has looked favorably on his people!"

Within these and other biblical narratives we become aware of the receptive hospitality which resides within the heart of Jesus. It is this kind of welcome and availability that resides at the core of missional hospitality. As God continues to work within us, we learn over time to see as Jesus sees.

The Good News is that Jesus moves beyond and between the divisions within society. See Luke 5:27-32 where Jesus:

> ...saw a tax collector named Levi, sitting at a tax booth; and he said to him, 'Follow me' and he got up, left everything, and followed him. Then Levi gave a great banquet for him in his house; and there was a large crowd of tax collectors and others sitting at the table with them. The Pharisees . . . were complaining . . . saying, 'Why do you eat and drink with tax collectors and sinners?' Jesus answered, 'Those who are well have no need of a physician, but those who are sick; I have come to call not the righteous but sinners to repentance.'

Even Simon Peter resists God's invitation to include persons who have not followed the Mosaic law. To prepare Peter for ministry in the home of Cornelius, a Roman centurion, God gives him a vision of animals and creatures which, according to the Mosaic Law, are unclean, and therefore unacceptable for food. But God tells Peter to "kill and eat." The vision is given three times, and each time Peter refuses the command, saying, "By no means, Lord; for I have never eaten anything that is profane or unclean." God tells Peter, "What God has made clean, you must not call profane" (Acts 10).

As we begin living into the Great Story of God we are called to see people of all kinds, of all ages, of all social backgrounds, differently: to see persons as Jesus sees them. Out of this seeing, we learn to live differently. Paul writes in 2 Cor. 5:16-19:

> From now on, therefore, we regard no one from a human point of view; . . . So if anyone is in Christ, there is a new creation: . . . see, everything has become new! All this is from God, who reconciled us to himself through Christ, and has given us the ministry of reconciliation; that is, in Christ God was reconciling the world to himself, not counting their trespasses against them.

For Your Reflection

The world's system sets up its own way of seeing and judging. Reflect on some of the ways this kind of seeing and judging is prevalent with our western world and in your world:

Reflect on how you see people. What responses are you aware of within yourself?

As you get in touch with how you see and respond, what biblical narrative do you identify with?

What is God's invitation to you here?

As you connect – in person and in other ways – you are invited to share with your small group about how you are practicing this spiritual discipline of hospitality through:

Participation in worship

Fellowship

Mission

Make a note of what you are learning from others in your group, and what gifts and guidance you have to offer.

Background Readings:

Heath and Kisker. *Longing for Spring: A New Vision for Wesleyan Community.* Chapter 6 "Reports from the Horizon". 61 – 69.
Schools for Conversion: 12 Marks of the New Monasticism. Mark 3: "Hospitality to the Stranger". 39 – 54.
Miller, Wendy. *Invitation to Presence: A Guide to Spiritual Disciplines.* Ch.6. 71 – 85. Guidance for Practice.
Heath and Kisker. Appendix B. Contains a series of schedules for weekly group meetings, designed to be used by small groups for a six-week spiritual formation and discernment process. 86 – 96.

6
Living the New Monastic Rule: Gifts

We will honor and care for the gift of the earth and its resources.
Practicing ecologically responsible living
Striving for simplicity rather than excessive consumption

We will practice generosity
In sharing our material resources
Including money
Within and beyond this community

We will use our spiritual gifts, talents, and abilities
To serve God
Within and beyond this community

+ WE WILL HONOR AND CARE FOR THE GIFT OF THE EARTH AND ITS RESOURCES, PRACTICING ECOLOGICALLY RESPONSIBLE LIVING. STRIVING FOR SIMPLICITY RATHER THAN EXCESSIVE CONSUMPTION +

Scott A. Bessenecker says,

> We are spitting pollutants into the air, water and soil like never before, forests are disappearing while deserts are encroaching on fertile land, there's a hole in the ozone, and we can't dig landfills quickly enough to dispose of all the Styrofoam cups and baby diapers we keep going through. . . . We are using up our planet and the world's poor are feeling it most.[25]

Our planet is being used, used up. We do not stop to appreciate the earth as a gift, sustaining our lives and well-being. Rather, it is one more commodity to be consumed.

If we are to live into a new monasticism, then we are called to be present, to pay attention to the earth we tread. To help us disconnect from the unconscious hold of consumer lifestyle in the west, Bessenecker offers "Suggestions for Simple Living." (181 – 183) His suggestions offer further guidance to us as we seek to live into the new monastic rule of giving honor and care for the gift of the earth and its resources practicing ecologically responsible living striving for simplicity rather than excessive consumption.

Relationship
Cultivate a relationship with God.
Practice regular hospitality.
Help each other, emphasize service.
Don't judge.
Reject anything that breeds the oppression of others.
Consciously seek to identify with the poor and forgotten. Start by visiting hospitals, prisons and nursing homes.
Schedule "simple" dates with your significant other.

---

[25] Bessenecker, Scott A. *The New Friars: The Emerging Movement Serving the World's Poor* (IVP Books, 2006). Pp. 158 – 59.

Activities
Make your commitments simple.
Don't overwork.
Fast periodically from media, food, people.
Simplify Christmas and other holidays. Develop the habit of homemade celebrations.

Pace and Atmosphere
Slow down.
Lie fallow.
Say no.

Possessions and Finances
Cultivate contentment, desire less.
Learn to enjoy things without owning them. Benefit from places of "common ownership" (parks, museums, libraries, rivers, public beaches).
De-accumulate.
Avoid impulse buying.
Learn how to make do with a lower income instead of needing a higher one.

Appreciation
Be grateful for things great and small.
Appreciate creation.

Spiritual Life
Meditate on Scripture.
Pray.
Encourage simple worship.

Appreciating Creation

We live this side of Eden, on this side of Genesis 3. The shining, pulsating and fruitful Earth which hung in full readiness for the words: "Let us make humankind in our image, according to our likeness; . . . "and was present as God created humankind in his image, in the image of God he created them; male and female were they created. God blessed them, and God said to them, "Be fruitful and multiply, and fill the earth . . . See, I have given you every plant yielding seed that is upon the face of all the earth, and every tree with seed in its fruit; you shall have them for food . . . God saw everything that he had made, and indeed, it was very good. (Genesis 1:26 – 31)

But then came another voice, the lie was spun and was believed, and the knowledge of good and evil – under the deadly mask of making one wise and God-like – now infiltrates the lives of the first man and the first woman. Creation also feels the sting of the lie. We hear God describing to us the condition of this once-fruitful planet: "Cursed is the ground because of you (the man); in toil you shall eat of it all the days of your life; thorns and thistles it shall bring forth for you; . . . by the sweat of your face you shall eat bread." (Genesis 3:17b – 19a)

When the first son of Adam and Eve grows jealous of his brother because of how he worships, God warns him about his anger, but Cain does not listen. Instead, in rage he kills his brother Abel, and buries his body in the ground. When the Lord asks him, "Where is your brother Abel?" Cain says, "I do not know; am I my brother's keeper?" And the Lord says, "What have you done" listen; your brother's blood is crying out to me from the ground!. . ." The ground of the earth houses murdered bodies, holds their blood, and cries out. Creation speaks, even groans, "waiting with eager longing . . . for the creation was subjected to futility." (Romans 8:19-20). Creation loses its purpose, and longs to be set free from its bondage to decay. . . . "We know that the whole creation has been groaning in labor pains until now . . ." (Romans 8:19 – 22).

As we walk, as we stand and sit still, as we gaze, and pay attention to creation, we are to listen. God still tends, God still provides, creation still cradles our lives and grows our food, still shines in beauty. At the same time, creation groans – bearing the weight of countless bodies of those who die because of violence: murder, slaughter, war, ravages of disease, and starvation. And creation groans, waiting for God to make all things new for resurrection.

Pay attention to creation. Creation also groans as it bears the weight of poison and pollution, the rape of its forests, the contamination of its waters, the extinction of some species of birds, fish, mammals because we have consumed the fruit of the earth with no thought of her bounty being a living gift to be held and enjoyed in gratitude.

Our 'consumer economy' lives and thrives off the anxiety of its victims, we who always fear there will never be enough; who will not shop if the shelves are not full; who can never have enough; who work and enjoy no leisure – giving up paid vacations because "there is not enough time to take a vacation." Worry invades the fabric of our lives, woven into the fabric of consumer culture.

For Your Reflection

Take some unhurried time to read Matthew 6: 25 – 34, twice.

Pay attention to those words or phrases that stand out to you as you read.

Now, go outside. Take some time to be in God's creation. Walk slowly. Be still. Be present – with eyes and ears open. Simply be there.

Gaze. Listen. Walk. Notice.

Listen again to the words of Jesus:

> Look at the birds of the air; they neither sow nor reap nor gather into barns, and yet your heavenly Father feeds them. And are you not of more value than they? . . .
> Consider the lilies of the field, how they grow; they neither toil nor spin, yet I tell you, even Solomon in all his glory was not clothed like one of these. . . . if God so clothes the grass

of the field, . . . will he not much more clothe you – you of little faith?

Therefore do not worry, saying, 'What will we eat?' or 'What will we drink?' or 'What will we wear?' For it is the Gentiles who strive for all these things; and indeed your heavenly Father knows that you need all these things.
But strive first for the kingdom of God and his righteousness, and all these things will be give to you as well. (Matthew 6:26-33)

As we gaze – look upon and contemplate – God's creation, we become aware of God's care and provision. Our stress and worry, our striving come to rest. And we are drawn into the deeper and wider space of God's gracious realm and God's provision and care; the giftedness in it all.

What do you notice as you take some time to be in creation – and in the presence of God who sustains all that is?

What are your worries?

What do you strive for?

What does Jesus call you to strive for?

Covenant Questions

In what way have you honored and cared for the earth and its gift of resources?

How have you practiced responsible living, striving for simplicity rather than excessive consumption?

+ WE WILL PRACTICE GENEROSITY IN SHARING OUR MATERIAL RESOURCES INCLUDING MONEY WITHIN AND BEYOND OUR COMMUNITY +

We are called again to join the early believers in their practice of generosity, sharing material resources. Turn to Acts 2:43 – 47, and 4:32 – 37. Read these two passages again – twice, slowly.

Enter in to these narratives.
Join these early followers of Jesus as they:

sell their possessions in order to provide for the poor and needy among them

worship and pray together

break bread together around table in their homes

eat food with gladness and joy together

praise God.

What do you notice?

What catches your attention?

For Your Reflection

The following questions may help you get in touch with where and how you learned your present attitude towards, and use of, money.

What attitude toward money and possessions did you learn

. . . in your family of origin?

. . . in school, or college?

. . . in your place(s) of employment?

. . . from the world around you?

. . . from your friends?

. . . from the church?

What is still a challenge for you?

Covenant Questions

In what way have you practiced generosity in sharing your material resources, including money, within and beyond your community?

+ WE WILL USE OUR SPIRITUAL GIFTS, TALENTS, AND ABILITIES TO SERVE GOD WITHIN AND BEYOND OUR COMMUNITY +

Somehow to speak of spiritual gifts – something that is given to us -- flies in the face of our modern world's dictum which shapes and controls our life, our belief that "life happens only if we make it happen." How could talents and abilities be gifts, and what on earth is a spiritual gift? What kind of talk is that? Aren't we getting a bit 'off' here? Maybe 'crazy'?

If we turn back to the first two chapters of Genesis again, we learn that we did not 'make ourselves,' but rather that all that is made is a gift – a gift of God's love, creativity, and generosity. God is the maker of life. We do not make life happen. We also learn – from chapter 3 on – what we have done with that gift, once the lie took up residence within and among us. Hence our anxiety, our bent towards holding on to what we have, rather than resting into God's great giving and provision, and seeing our talents, our abilities, and yes, our spiritual gifts – to serve the good of others, near and far.

Yes, following Jesus – responding to him saying to us, "Come with me" – meets us on this level too. But that is exactly what makes this following Jesus authentic: it meets us on Monday mornings, on all week days, and nights, and meets us wherever we are, no matter which street we are walking, or persons we meet. As we follow Jesus around in the gospels, we discover how he is present, how he lives his life – not as something to be grasped, but as a gift.

Before Jesus ascended back into heaven, he gathered all of his followers around him and told them to wait for the coming of the Holy Spirit – the One who would be their Helper, Guide, Teacher, and Advocate (see John 14). With the coming of the Spirit on the day of Pentecost, these early believers found themselves gifted and empowered in ways they had not known before. Paul, the apostle to the Gentiles, writes to the believers and members of the house churches in Corinth, explaining how the Holy Spirit gives a variety of spiritual gifts for the purpose of the common good. In the letter to the church in Ephesus, the writer again speaks of gifts given by the resurrected Christ – gifts which equip believers for the work of ministry and which build up the body of Christ. A close reading of I

Corinthians 12 and 13, Romans 12, and Ephesians 4 help us get in touch again with giftedness. We do not do the work of serving God alone. The apostle Paul became aware that as we do the work of God, the Holy Spirit is at work in those we serve. He mentions this in his letter to the house churches in Thessalonica (1:5,6).

For Your Reflection

Take some time to read, slowly, prayerfully, the following section of St. Paul's letter to the believers in Philippi – the first European city to receive the good news of the gospel. There are tensions between some of the persons in leadership among the house churches, and so Paul writes and offers guidance, spiritual guidance. Rather than being impractical, this kind of guidance touches into the fabric of every-day living and our relationship as we walk and live together, as we follow Jesus:

> If there is any encouragement in Christ,
> any consolation from love,
> any sharing in the Spirit,
> any compassion and sympathy,
> make each other's joy complete:
> be of the same mind, having the same love
> being in full accord and of one mind.
> Do nothing from selfish ambition or conceit
> but in humility regard others as better than yourselves.
> Let each of you look not to your own interests,
> but to the interests of others.
> Let the same mind be in you that was in Christ Jesus,
> who, thought he was in the form of God,
> did not regard equality with God as something to be exploited,
> but emptied himself,
> taking the form of a slave,
> being born in human likeness.
> And being found in human form,
> he humbled himself
> and became obedient to the point of death –
> even death on a cross.
> Therefore God also highly exalted him
> and gave him the name that is above every name.
> So that at the name of Jesus every knee should bend,
> in heaven and on earth and under the earth,
> and every tongue should confess
> that Jesus Christ is Lord,
> to the glory of God the Father.
> (Philippians 2:2 – 11)

Covenant Questions

In the last week or two:

In what way have you used your spiritual gifts, talents and abilities to serve God within and beyond the community you live and walk with?

For Your Prayer Practice

A spiritual discipline which helps us get in touch with how we are living this pilgrimage of loving and following Jesus, loving our neighbor as we love ourselves, and being mindful of God's gifts in us, and in creation, is rooted in the Hebrew Scriptures, and over time became more structured in the Jesuit Order in the 16th Century. Often called the "consciousness examen", this prayer form is not an examination which will be graded, nor an X-ray of our conscience. Rather, this prayerful reflection helps us become aware of our inner and outer responses across the day – to God, to others, to ourselves, and to creation.

It is helpful to include the practice of the Consciousness Examen either at the end of the day, or at the end of the week. Have your journal alongside, and make a note of what stands out for you, what God's invitation is to you as you reflect prayerfully with the guidance of the Holy Spirit.

Restoring the Soul in Service and Mission: The Consciousness Examen

Be still. Allow your body to be at rest.
Release any tension. Your body is a good friend; appreciate this gift of God.

Open your attention to God prayerfully; and invite the Holy Spirit to help you see your day/week as God does.

Reflection
Look back over the last day/24 hours or week.
Let the events unfold and pass before you.
What emerges? What persons or events stand out for you?

For what are you thankful?

For what are you least thankful?

Whose story did you listen to?

In what ways are you aware of the presence of God in those you listened to?

What attitudes do you notice within yourself?

. . . anxiety, anger, sadness, fear, guilt, hostility . . .?

. . . faith (your response to God, those times when you turned to God)?

. . . hope (your response in the face of difficulties, stressors)?

. . . love (your attitude and response towards yourself and towards others, towards creation)?

. . . joy (what energized you and brought you joy, satisfaction)?

In what ways did you meet God in your responses?

In what ways did you miss God?

Prayer

Ask the Holy Spirit to help you as you come into the presence of God/Jesus now.

Bring your needs to God.

Bring the needs of others you have listened to into the presence of God.

End this time of prayerful reflection by simply
resting in the presence of God/Jesus/Holy Spirit.

For Your Reflection

Which insight had particular significance for you?

What surfaced that you would like to stay with, and pray about again?

ADDITIONAL READING

Jonathan Wilson-Hartgrove, New Monasticism: What it has to say to Today's Church. Brazos Press, 2008.

Scott A. Bessenecker, *The New Friars: The Emerging Movement Serving the World's Poor.* Ch.10 "Our Darkest Hour" and Appendix A: Suggestions for Simple Living.

7

Living the New Monastic Rule: Service

We will serve God and neighbor out of gratitude and love for God

We will practice mutual accountability with a covenant group for how we serve God and neighbor

We will practice regular Sabbath as a means of renewal so that can we can lovingly serve God and neighbor

+ WE WILL SERVE GOD AND NEIGHBOR OUT OF GRATITUDE AND LOVE FOR GOD. +

In the gospel narratives we discover that the followers of Jesus did not always serve him out of gratitude or love. And in the spiritual writings across the life of the church, we find the same theme. This side of Eden our motives are mixed; we are driven by our old nature in our self-serving choices, and we are led by the Spirit of God into God-centered choices.

In the days before his arrest, trial, and crucifixion Jesus spoke several times to his close followers about what lay ahead for him – and for them. Since they fully expected him to become the triumphal Messiah, such a prediction just did not fit their expectations. They saw Jesus as the One who would rescue the nation of Israel from the occupation by the Roman Empire, who would restore the nation's fortune, who would remove the self-serving king and ascend to the throne of Israel. To think otherwise seemed impossible. To think otherwise filled them with fear.

All through those days and nights leading up to his death, Jesus assured these early disciples that this death he was about to suffer would not be the end. He would come back from the dead. He would be resurrected. And after all those tragic events are over, and the resurrection a reality, he tells them he will meet with them in Galilee. Jesus promises to join them on the shores of the lake they know so well, the place where Jesus had called them together to be with him on retreat, away from the busy and distorted epicenters of the world around them. And so we find the disciples making the long walk from Jerusalem to Capernaum – some 90 miles – in order to meet Jesus by the lake.

They invite us to join them as dawn spills its light across the dark waters of the lake. Enter the narrative prayerfully as you read John 21 in the following guided meditation:

A charcoal fire glows on the shore. Our gospel companions have been fishing all night—a fishing expedition initiated by Simon Peter. They are still in the boat when a voice calls to them from the shore: "Children, you have no fish, have you?" They had been fishing all night and had caught nothing. Now, this one standing on the shore calls to them again, "Cast your net to the right side of the boat, and you will find some." So they cast their net, and now they are not able to haul it in because there are so many fish. It is John who recognizes this one standing on the shore: "It is the Lord!" he shouts.

With sudden joy and relief, Simon grabs his tunic, jumps into the lake and swims to shore. The smell of fish roasting on the charcoal fire greets him as he wades out of the water. Then comes a kind invitation from Jesus: "Come and have breakfast."

Here Jesus serves as host as well as cook. He comes to these men in this familiar place beside the lake, offering comfort for body and for soul. After breakfast he asks Simon to walk with him along the shore; Simon who a few days earlier had denied he ever knew this Jesus, who swore he was not one of his   followers. Jesus opens the conversation: "Simon son of John, do you love me more than these?" Simon replies, "Yes, Lord; you know that I love you." Jesus is not inquiring about Simon's strength. He is not asking for Simon's five-year goals. He does not mention Simon's betrayal. He does not discuss this man's habit of being the first to speak, often first to initiate action, and who repeatedly falls and fails. This is instead a conversation about loving.

The setting of this exchange – early dawn, a charcoal fire -- evokes Simon's memories of his fear and weakness, those times when he caught a glimpse of his interior self. Jesus is evoking Simon's awareness and ownership of what Simon would perceive as weakness in himself. Jesus is inviting Simon to turn inward, to become intimate with himself – an act of self-love and acceptance – as he owns and feels his vulnerability.

Jesus asks this disciple a second time, "Simon son of John, do you love me?" There is no mention of Peter here, rather an invitation to Simon to remember his human origin, to own his humanity rather than being caught up in the façade of a rock-like leader. Again Simon replies, "Yes, Lord . . . " "Tend my sheep," Jesus says in response.

Then Jesus asks again, a third time, "Simon son of John, do you love me?" This insistent questioning finally penetrates Simon's tough exterior and finds its way into the great heart and soul of this man. Peter begins to feel pain: the pain of not always being able to succeed—even as a fisherman; the pain of knowing he did not measure up to the gracious holiness that permeated the being of Jesus; the pain of knowing he had boasted of great loyalty to the Messiah but at the hint of threat had denied even knowing him. Finally, he is able to stay with his pain, to be with himself—human, weak, fallible, limited, sinful. Jesus had stayed with him all across these years and walks beside him now—just as he is. "Lord, you know everything: you know that I love you."

Yes, Jesus does know everything about him. Now Simon Peter is beginning to know himself even as he is known. He has come home to himself and home to God in a new way. A new intimacy is emerging within his mind and being. This self-awareness, an inner transparency to stay present to himself rather than to adopt a strong but false front, will enable him to be present to God and to do what Jesus calls him to do: "Feed my sheep."

On through the centuries of the church, spiritual writers discover and write to this same theme: loving God. Bernard of Clairvaux, an abbot in the Cistercian order during the twelfth century, offers spiritual guidance about loving. He says that first we love ourselves for our own sake. While this kind of love can be self-centered and narcissistic, it is needful for us to love and be protective and caring of ourselves – to know ourselves as lovable. Then we begin over time in our young lives to realize that there is someone beyond our self – and we begin to seek God. Our love begins to change and grow; we learn to love God as useful and necessary. We love God because God provides what we need. Simon Peter had come to know Jesus in this way—as the Messiah who fed the multitude, stilled storms on the lake, who healed the sick. And, yes, Simon Peter had also expected Jesus to claim the throne of David and restore the nation of Israel. When this latter expectation did not become reality, Simon's love and loyalty faltered. He had not yet been able to grow in his experience and practice of loving God because of who God is, not because of what God is able to do for him. Now Jesus is drawing Simon Peter to love God for God's sake.

Later Simon Peter would be tending the flock, feeding the sheep of God's pasture, the new believers who also found themselves faced by threat of accusation, imprisonment, and even death because they had come to know Jesus as the Messiah. These early believers leave Jerusalem, and scatter throughout the Roman Empire. And Peter is able to write letters of guidance and encouragement to them, speaking of the enormous capacity of love to embrace and to stay with the weakness and sin within people. He would advise these followers of Jesus above all to maintain constant love for one another, for love covers a multitude of sins; to be hospitable to one another without complaining. Like good stewards of the manifold grace of God, to serve one another with whatever gift each person has received. (See 1 Peter 1:1 - 9; 4:8 – 11)

For Your Reflection

We have a tendency to look back over our lives and notice where we have sinned or fallen short of God's call on our lives. Our gospel companions remember the many times when Jesus noticed and named the presence of faith, hope, and love in people's lives. In the New Testament letters we discover the writers affirming the faith, hope, and love being lived out in the lives of believers. The Consciousness Examen is a spiritual discipline that offers guidance as we reflect on how faith, hope, and love guide us in our inward and outward daily living and service.

The Consciousness Examen

Preparation
Ask the Holy Spirit to help you see your life across the last day/week.

Reflection
Look back over the last day (or week). Let the events unfold and pass before you. What emerges? What persons or events stand out for you?

What attitudes do you notice within yourself as you reflect on what drives you, or who leads you as you are present for God, and as you serve others?

Anxiety, anger, sadness, fear, guilt, hostility, grief, other emotions

Faith: responding to God

Hope: responding in hope in the face of difficulties

Love: responding in love to God, to your self and to others

Gratitude: simply being thankful – to God, to others
Where are these attitudes taking you?

Towards God, your self, others?

Away from God, your self, others?

Be in the presence of Jesus now. Just as Jesus walked the shore with Simon, so be with Jesus as he walks the shore of your life.

Bring your needs, your thanks, your confession, your petitions. Know that you are heard, loved, forgiven, and restored.

Bring your gratitude and simply rest in the presence of this One who knows and loves you.

Hear the words of the Apostle Paul – previously Saul who had hated Jesus, and all who followed him; Saul who had persecuted the church. But Jesus met him, and called this Saul to know truly who Jesus is, and to serve him:

You were called to freedom, brothers and sisters; only do not use your freedom as an opportunity for self- indulgence, but through love become servants to one another. For the whole law is summed up in a single commandment, 'You shall love your neighbor as yourself.' . . . Bear one another's burdens, and in this way you will fulfill the law of Christ. (Gal. 5:13-14; 6:2)

+ WE WILL PRACTICE MUTUAL ACCOUNTABILITY WITH A COVENANT GROUP FOR HOW WE SERVE GOD AND NEIGHBOR +

The rhythm of coming, being with Jesus, receiving soul care and guidance for engagement in ministry, then being sent out, is part of the rhythm and rule of Jesus' followers. Included in this rhythm and rule of life and ministry, Jesus arranges for times of drawing away with the disciples for private conversation, retreat for rest, reporting in, prayer, and spiritual guidance. The gospel narrators invite us to sit in on their practice of mutual accountability for how they serve God and neighbor. As we do so we become part of their covenant group.

While these gospel companions say little of their own experience of outward ministry, they do draw our attention to several times when they return from ministry and re-gather around Jesus. (See Mark 6:30 – 32; Luke 9:10; and Mathew 11:28 – 30)

This rhythm of coming and being with one another, of being sent, and then of returning to be with one another again can become a model for our own lives and ministry. Attention to re-gathering, to checking in, to rest, and receiving soul-care and guidance for ministry can then inform the shape and content of our time together.

Return and Regathering

On their return "the apostles gathered around Jesus" (Mark 6:30).

The return is marked by coming—to be with Jesus and with one another. This is a time of opening one's attention to Jesus and to the others present.

We can come to a meeting so full of our own agendas that we have little space for God or other persons present. As a result, we forget the intent for our return and re-gathering. This place of meeting offers attention to the intent of receiving rest and renewal.

Reporting In

They told him all they had done and taught (Mark 6:30).

Our gospel companions note that part of this re-gathering is given to telling Jesus and each other all they had done and taught. A kind of ministry report is given here. Luke and Mark offer us a verbatim of some of these conversations. See Luke 10:17 – 24 and Mark 9:17 – 18.

Receiving Ministry Supervision and Spiritual Guidance

> The seventy returned with joy saying,
> "Lord, in your name even the demons submit to us!"
> (Luke 10:17)

Seeing the larger dimension

First Jesus sets their particular work of ministry within the larger picture and context of kingdom and heavenly realities: "I watched Satan fall from heaven like a flash of lightning." Here Jesus reveals to us that evil is losing its power as we engage in ministry. Our acts of ministry can seem small, insignificant, and earthbound. But ministry in the name of Jesus is a sign of the kingdom of God—the gracious rule of heaven showing up among us, here and now.

Remembering the Source of Authority

Jesus continues by directing the disciples' attention to the source of this authority. We serve "in the name of Jesus." It is Jesus who has given us this authority. He goes on to say, ". . . nothing will hurt you."

This authority is a gift. We are dependent on God, on Jesus, on the presence and work of the Holy Spirit in all that we do. Here we also catch the reassurance Jesus gives as he calls his disciples into this ministry of confronting the powers. As the apostle Paul learned, "Be strong in the Lord and in the strength of his power. Put on the whole armor of God, so that you may be able to stand against the wiles of the devil. For our struggle is not against enemies of blood and flesh, but against the rulers, against the authorities, against the cosmic powers of this present darkness, against spiritual forces of evil in the heavenly places" (Ephesians 6:10 – 12).

The "push-back" we experience in ministry may come from various sources, and can evoke a certain fear, anxiety, and discouragement within us. But as we meet with our covenant group, to check in, to share, to be accountable to each other, we also discern the source of our fear, our anxiety, and any discouragement. As we settle into God's presence together, the Spirit of Jesus renews our soul, settles us back into that restful center, and helps us remember in Whose name and authority we serve.

Discerning the source of joy

These disciples are reveling in the amount of power and authority they have received. Any kind of power can be seductive. Spiritual power can also entice. Jesus directs their attention to a deeper source of joy: not power over demons (or other powers of human standing), but rather their identity as children of God. They belong to the family of God, and their names are written in the birth records of heaven. Our identity is given us. We are children of God. We belong in God's household. When this reality sinks deep into our awareness, we can loosen our grip on our need to prove ourselves, to being in control; we become aware of the deceptive lure of our desire for domination. Jesus is calling us to change our understanding of power. The source of our joy is discerned, challenged, and redirected.

Love, I will love you Lord, with all my heart,
O Lord I will tell the wonder of your ways
And magnify your Name.
Love, I will love you Lord, with all my heart,
In you I will find the source of all my joy,
Alleluia.[26]

For Your Reflection

In what way do you return and re-gather with a covenant group?

to share your life and ministry together

to share your experience of living into the new monastic rule of life

to remember the larger dimension of the kingdom now and coming
in which you live and serve

to remember that you serve in Jesus' name, and find in him the
source of your joy.

to be present to God with each other, and to seek guidance and
discernment, and spiritual direction together

to pray with and for each other, and to bless each other

---

[26] Fraysee, Cluade. "Praise, I Will Praise You, Lord." (No. 26). *A Worship Book.* trans Morse, Kenneth J. Mennonite and Brethren Publishing, 1992.

+ WE WILL PRACTICE REGULAR SABBATH AS A MEANS OF RENEWAL SO THAT CAN WE CAN LOVINGLY SERVE GOD AND NEIGHBOR+

The danger we fall into is that as servants of the Gospel, we forget that we need Sabbath and rest. However, if we follow Jesus in the gospels, we will soon learn that Jesus often "went out to a deserted place" for time in solitude, rest, and prayer. Sometimes he took his followers with him.

What is it about retreat, about deserted places – wilderness – that draws us into Sabbath and rest? And what are we resting from? In our western world – and in many other parts of the world – the need to produce, to make money, to be a success, drives us. We keep on the move, in the unconscious belief that everything is up to us. We become busy, frustrated, tired, anxious, and when we do stop, we want to escape – to get away from it all. The pace of life is exhausting and stressful, and we often turn to something to numb the pain of this unrelenting marathon.

Sabbath is restorative, draws us into rest, and opens us up to the reality that we do not make life happen. Life is a gift, created and given by God, the God who sustains and stays with us. Our work becomes seen more as vocation, and we begin embracing a rhythm of work and Sabbath rest, rather than the drivenness of production and the need to escape.

Because we are so accustomed to action, doing, production, we will find it hard to stop. We may ask, "What are we going to do?" We find ourselves experiencing a kind of withdrawal, a desire to avoid the seeming emptiness of rest and not-doing. We are more attached and addicted to work and production than we realize. We do not shift easily into Sabbath rest.

This is not just a present-day problem. In the twelfth century Bernard of Clairvaux wrote a series of letters (which became five short books entitled *On Consideration*) to Eugenius III, a former monk in the monastic community of Clairvaux. Bernard continues as his spiritual director and writes to remind Eugenius to take time for prayerful reflection and meditation within the many demands of his new sphere of ministry as pope. Bernard is calling Eugenius into Sabbath.

He writes:
"If you wish to belong altogether to other people, like him (Jesus) who was made all things to all men, I praise your humanity, but only on condition that it be complete. But how can it be complete if you yourself are left out? You, too, are a man. So then, in order that your humanity may be entire and complete, let your bosom, which receives all, find room for yourself also. . . . In short if a man is bad to himself, to whom is he good? . . . (S)et aside some portion of your heart and of your time for consideration. . . . What is so essential to the worship of God as the practice to which He exhorts ion the Psalm, "Be still and know that I am God." This certainly is the chief object of consideration."

For Your Reflection

How good are you to yourself? In what way are your arranging the flow of your life and work schedule to include times and spaces for:

solitude?

prayer?

worship with others?

spiritual reading?

reflection / consideration?

restful leisure?

play?

8
Living the New Monastic Rule: Witness

We will practice racial and gender reconciliation

We will resist evil and injustice

We will pursue peace with justice

We will share the redeeming, healing,
creative love of God
In word
In deed
In presence
In order to invite others to Christian discipleship.

Jesus Reorders Our Lives

As we follow Jesus through the gospels and in our lives we find ourselves called into the new order. Increasingly we become conscious of how our lives till now were shaped by the old order. By new order I refer to Jesus' repeated statement, "You have heard it said, but I say unto you…"[27] Jesus interrupts our habitual thoughts and reactions, inviting us to a new way of being. That is, he "re-orders" our life. One spiritual discipline which leads us into seeing Jesus in action is a contemplative reading of the gospels. Below is an example of how to do this. As you will discover, the story of Bartimaeus (Mark 10:46-52) encompasses all the aspects of the rule of life concerning witness.

Jesus and his followers come now to the city of Jericho – a walled city about five miles west of the River Jordan – on their long walk south to Jerusalem. A crowd also walks the road as they come closer to the great city, on its way to celebrate the Passover. Passover is the high feast, a time for remembering and entering into the feast of unleavened bread; remembering and entering into their narrative of the "Great Escape" as Yahweh frees the children of Israel from slavery in Egypt.

Jesus is in the midst of this moving stream of men, women, and children, causing excited chatter. So much so that Bartimaeus, a blind beggar who is sitting near the city gate of Jericho, hears the noise, and asks what is happening. Some standing nearby tell him, "Jesus of Nazareth is passing by."

Bartimaeus has heard of this man Jesus. Other travelers as they make their way through the city of Jericho, talk of him and the wonders Jesus performs. Healing the deaf and the blind; the feeding of the five thousand; casting out demons, healing the lame and the sick.

On hearing that this Jesus is close by, Bartimaeus begins to shout, "Jesus, Son of David, have mercy on me!"
Those standing in front try to silence him. They sternly order him to

---

[27] Matthew 5 contains several of these references.

be quiet, wanting Bartimaeus to remain silent and invisible. In their eyes he is his affliction. They believe he is cursed by God. Caught within the confines of their own "order"—the way their world is supposed to work—they are deaf and blind to his humanity. They cannot see or hear the needs and the desires of their neighbor sitting outside the city wall, yelling for help.

But Bartimaeus has heard whispers of a new "order" – of One who listens to needy beggars and lepers, children and widows, the blind, the lame and the demon-possessed. And so in spite of their command to be quiet, he shouts even more loudly, "Son of David, have mercy on me!"

The multitude on the road hears his cries. They keep moving. But Jesus lives within the freedom of the new order. He listens to these shouts, and stands still. Then he speaks a new command: "Call him here." Jesus compels the people standing in front of this blind beggar, the very people who had ordered him to be quiet, to bring Bartimaeus to him. Now a new order—the way of Jesus--unfolds.

Suddenly, these bystanders wake up. They notice this blind beggar, listen to his shouts for help, and reach out to bring him to Jesus. In the new order the poor, the blind, the unnoticed, the needy are given place, are heard, are helped. The bystanders are no longer standing by. They say to Bartimaeus, "Take heart; get up, he is calling you." Bartimaeus throws off his beggar's cloak, and jumps up, and listens his way to Jesus.

Now -- as we join the crowd, stand still, watch, and listen -- Jesus becomes a servant to this blind beggar. Jesus asks him, "What do you want me to do for you?" Bartimaeus replies, "My teacher, let me see again." Jesus says to him, "Receive your sight; your faith has made you well."

Immediately, Bartimaeus regains his sight and follows Jesus, glorifying God. And all the people, when they see this, praise God.

For Your Reflection

If we are to walk in the way of Jesus, then we must form the habit of standing still, listening, seeing, and welcoming those persons whom we desire not to notice.

We need to grow in our hospitality of listening – both to our neighbors' shouts, and to their deeper needs. Gradually we learn to become a servant to the needy – even as Jesus becomes a servant to us, and helps us to walk the ways of this new "order"—the "order" of the kingdom of God.

What "old order" behavior are you aware of in your own life?

Who are the persons or people groups, which you would rather not notice?

In what way do you shut their shouts down, and order them to be quiet? Invisible?

In what way is the "new Order" of Jesus inviting you?
. . . to listen to their shouts and needs with the ears of Jesus?
. . . to see these persons with the eyes of Jesus, so that they come into focus, rather than being rendered invisible?
. . . to become aware of Jesus' presence with you as you notice, listen, and struggle to respond?

When Jesus asks you, "What do you want me to do for you?" how do you reply?

+ WE WILL PRACTICE GENDER AND RACIAL RECONCILIATION +

Jesus calls us to pay attention to how our culture forms us, and how that formation within various communities (family, gender, city, congregation, schools, nation, race, etc.) shapes our sense of identity and can bring us into harmony or conflict with others.

Racial and Societal Reconciliation

In the group of twelve Jesus called to himself, he included:

> Matthew the tax collector . . . (and) Simon the Cananaean who was called the Zealot. (Matthew 10:2-4; Luke 6:15)

In the time of Jesus, Simon the Zealot would be strongly against people who participated in any way with the Roman occupation of the nation of Israel. Matthew, a Jew who worked for the Roman Empire collecting taxes from his own people, was considered a traitor and an outcast. He was despised not only by Zealots (freedom fighters who used acts of terror to preserve the nation of Israel) but also by the Pharisees, strict religious leaders. In calling these two men to be part of the twelve, Jesus also calls them to examine their own personal history and narrative, and how their history could affect their sense of identity, belief systems, and community as his followers.

These two men begin to discover that the center of their lives needs to shift. For Simon the Cananaean, this means surrendering his zeal for national supremacy at all costs, and embracing the Way of Jesus. The shift refocuses Simon's desire towards the kingdom of God and God's Way of rescuing the world. For Matthew, it means giving up a well-paying job to follow and trust this rabbi Jesus. Through friendship with Jesus, these men are reconciled. Both men come to know their own belovedness. Now they enter into a life which will cost them everything, but will quench their deepest human and spiritual thirst. Now they will discover peace beyond anything the world's system can offer.

Gender reconciliation

As we follow Jesus in the gospels and learn to stand still and listen, we discover him engaging women with respect, empowerment, compassion, and hospitality.

One of the homes Jesus visits regularly is in Bethany, not far from Jerusalem. Two sisters live there – Mary and Martha – along with their brother Lazarus. Turn to Luke 10:38-42, and as you read, enter into the narrative. Know that you are invited in to their home, along with Jesus and his followers.

This is not a narrative about Mary's laziness, but rather about finding her center. Just as Matthew and Simon the Zealot needed to re-orient their lives around a transforming center, so Martha is called to do the same. Mary has found that center in Jesus. Martha's primary gift is service and hospitality. But as we follow her around the kitchen of her home, we are soon aware of how frustrated and angry she becomes. And the more troubled she becomes, the more distracted she is. Martha forgets the primary path and desire of her gift. She finds herself running to keep up as the many tasks multiply. Exploding into the living space, she complains: "Lord, do you not care . . . ?" She feels sorry for herself: ". . . my sister has left me to do all the work by myself." And she becomes controlling: "Tell her to help me!"

In response, Jesus speaks her name, twice, drawing Martha back into her true self. In this way he helps her discern her scattered and anxious condition: "Martha, Martha, you are worried and distracted by many things; there is need of only one thing. Mary has chosen the better part, which will not be taken away from her." The "one thing" that Martha needs is the "better part" that Mary has already found. Jesus both affirms Mary's choice, and tends Martha's need by calling her to center her life around God and God's gifts and desire for her life.

Later in the gospel narrative, six days before the great Passover feast at Jerusalem, we join Jesus and his followers again in Bethany. Jesus knows that his time has come to be handed over to the religious authorities, to be tried, condemned, beaten, and then crucified. One more time he finds refuge and an oasis of quiet and care in the home of Lazarus, Martha, and Mary. Turn to John 12:1-8. As you read, join Jesus in their home.

Dinner is being served by Martha. She is now centered and at ease as she serves the meal to this Rabbi, this friend, who has spoken openly about his death and resurrection. Mary also brings something into the room – perfume: a whole pound of precious and pure fragrance. As Jesus and his friends eat, she kneels at his feet and anoints them with the perfume, and then wipes his feet with her hair. The fragrance fills the house.

Judas Iscariot – who carries the common purse among the twelve disciples – complains: "Why was this perfume not sold for three hundred denarii (nearly a year's wages for a common laborer) and the money given to the poor?" The gospel commentary then notes that Judas does not care for the poor, but rather wants more money in the common purse – because he is a thief, and steals its contents. Jesus turns to Judas, and reprimands him: "Leave her alone. She bought it so that she might keep it for the day of my burial. You always have the poor with you, but you do not always have me."

Jesus reads Mary's heart, sees her inner knowing – and what moves her to anoint him for his death and burial. Mary sees what Judas – and even Jesus' other followers – could not and did not want to see. Martha serves in a way that others did not. And Lazarus sits at table. This family is at peace among themselves, and offer great depth of hospitality to Jesus and where he is on the road to Jerusalem and death.

In both of these narratives Jesus speaks light and guidance into the lives of Martha and Mary, affirming them, advocating for them, and welcoming with keen and loving discernment the gifts of love and service that each of them bring for him and other guests in their house.

In the lives of Mary and Martha and in many other gospel stories Jesus elevates the personhood and status of women in Jewish society, and so within the kingdom of God. As the followers of Jesus carry the stories of Jesus – the good news of the gospel – with them into the further reaches of the Roman Empire, they take this deepening respect for women with them. In a letter which the apostle Paul writes to the new believers in Galatia, about twenty years after Jesus' death and resurrection, we read,

> You . . . have clothed yourself with Christ. There is no longer Jew or Greek, there is no longer slave or free, there is no longer male and female; for all of you are one in Christ Jesus. (Galatians 3:27 – 28)

For Your Reflection

In what ways does your early and ongoing formation in your family of origin, in school, in the church, in the places where you have lived (village, town, city, country, nation) still shape and influence your response(s) in life and ministry:

Towards persons in the church?

Towards persons from other cultures?

Towards persons who are poor, homeless, rejected, needy?

Towards men? Towards women?

Towards persons with gifts that differ -- gifts we may not immediately recognize?

In what way does "love your neighbor" take on new meaning for you in light of this discussion?

+ WE WILL RESIST EVIL AND INJUSTICE +

Just as we become aware of our cultural, racial, and gender biases, so it takes time to become aware of what is evil, what is unjust. We may judge and punish a child for shoplifting milk in a grocery store – until we learn that his mother is a single parent, earning a minimum wage at her fulltime job, and has just paid the landlord the rent -- rent that has been raised for the third time in nine months, and which now devours two-thirds of her income. Who is the thief in this narrative? Practicing justice requires that we engage systems of oppression that result in children having to steal food to survive.

As we enter again into the temple in Jerusalem, we hear Jesus speaking out against the religious leaders. In this way Jesus resists evil and names injustice:

Woe to you, scribes and Pharisees, hypocrites! For you tithe mint, dill, and cumin and have neglected the weightier matters of the law: justice and mercy and faith. It is these you ought to have practiced without neglecting the others. You blind guides!

As he exposes their penchant for sitting in "the best seats in the synagogues and places of honor at banquets!" – so as to be seen as important by others. Jesus also calls these leaders to task because they "devour widows' houses" and "for the sake of appearance say long prayers." (Mark 12: 38 – 40)

It is the widows and the orphans, the poor and sick, that Jesus welcomes and calls us to care for. James, his brother, speaks to this in his letter:

Religion that is pure and undefiled before God, the Father, is this: to care for orphans and widows in their distress, and to keep oneself unstained by the world. (James 1:27)

Judgment to condemn

Jesus also insists that we pay attention to our own interior attitudes: our tendency to judge another, when we ourselves are also guilty. As we stay with Jesus on this gospel pilgrimage, we find ourselves in the temple at Jerusalem, early in the morning. This is the place where great crowds gather for the big festivals that mark God's presence and provision in their lives. As Jesus arrives a crowd soon forms around him and he sits down to teach. Turn to John 8: 1 – 11, and as you read, make your way into the temple.

As Jesus is teaching, some scribes and Pharisees come on the scene bringing a woman with them – a woman who has been caught in adultery -- and making her stand before all of them, they say to him, "Teacher, this woman was caught in the very act of committing adultery. Now in the law Moses commanded us to stone such women Now what do you say?"

(As we read this passage we may find ourselves wondering why only the woman was apprehended. What about the man she was with?)

Jesus says nothing in response to the question posed by the religious leaders, but he does make a statement. Bending over he starts writing with his finger on the ground. We are not told what he writes, but as we stand and watch, we see Jesus straightening himself up. In response to their repeated questioning he says, "Let anyone among you who is without sin be the first to throw a stone at her." Then once again he bends down and writes on the ground.

Gradually, one by one, beginning with the elders, these men and religious leaders leave. As we continue to watch, we realize that Jesus is left alone with the woman standing before him.

Jesus now stands up, and says to her, "Woman, where are they? Has no one condemned you?" And she says, "No one, sir." And then Jesus says to her, "Neither do I condemn you. Go your way, and from now on do not sin again."

As we learn the ways of Jesus, we discover how evil is exposed and resisted. This calls us to action, the kind of action that emerges out of uncovering the root of the problem. We are called to seek truth. And we are to meet the truth with love and kindness. Then kingdom justice happens. The kingdom comes among us and those we serve.

For Your Reflection

In what ways do you engage in resisting evil?

How do you participate in caring for the poor, the disenfranchised, orphans, widows, persons who are homeless?

+ WE WILL PURSUE PEACE WITH JUSTICE +

Sandra had finally decided to leave an abusive and terrorizing marriage. Her children were now adults, and she found the courage to make it on her own. Still suffering from the trauma of physical and emotional abuse, still experiencing panic attacks, she sought out the help of the medical world, also entered into counseling. But in order to get a place of her own, she needed to find a job. Scanning the Help Wanted ads in the local newspaper, Sandra noticed an ad for a home nurse assistant. That was a job she knew she could do, and would like. Sandra was a licensed certified nursing assistant, and had learned that she preferred to work in a private home rather than in a hospital or nursing home. Calling the phone number in the ad was another anxious moment for her, but she made the call, and while in conversation, wrote down the address for an interview. That afternoon, her hands shaking, feeling stressed and anxious, Sandra tried to follow the directions to the house. Taking a wrong turn, she found herself about to give up, but then remembered the steady, kind voice of the woman she had conversation with; and she decided to call again. Five minutes later Sandra found herself pulling into the driveway of a small house on the south side of town.

The interview went well despite all her fears, and Sandra got the job. However, soon she found herself overcome with panic attacks. The work was not difficult. And the woman she was caring for was kind and understanding. But Sandra felt stressed and walked off the job, not just once, but five times. She knew she would lose her job, but somehow the panic and trauma took control of reason.

When her cell phone rang, she fully expected to be fired. But instead, Mrs. Mullins asked her to return. "I know all about panic attacks," Mrs. Mullins explained to Sandra. "Instead of walking out, sit down and take a deep breath, then come and talk to me. I know you're in counseling, and seeing a doctor. That's very important. But it's also very important that you stay on the job too. I need you here. I was about to fire you, but then I prayed about it, and Jesus told me to keep you on. You see, Jesus reminded me of how much I was like you when I was younger, and working – sometimes as a nursing assistant. I did not do relationships well, and when panic took over, I had a habit of walking away. So, after praying, I decided to let you stay, and not fire you. There's some things we're going to work at, but for now, go and fix my dinner, honey; I'm hungry."

Sandra, her smile bathed in tears of relief, thanked Mrs. Mullins and went back into the kitchen to start fixing her evening meal. As she carried the tray into the room where Mrs. Mullins, disabled and unable to walk, spent most of her day. Mrs. Mullins handed her a note book and a ballpoint, and said, "Here, this is for you. While I'm eating, I want you to write some things down. First, write on one page why you should get fired. Then on another page, write the reasons why you should keep the job. And then, on a third page, write down a list of things you want to pay attention to in your own life, ways you want to grow stronger in and improve. And don't think I came up with all this wisdom on my own," she said with a grin. "Jesus told me what he wants you to write."

Sandra liked writing. That was one thing she could do well, and as Mrs. Mullins enjoyed chicken noodle soup, fruit salad, and a roll, Sandra began to write. After she was done she and Mrs. Mullins looked over her lists together, and then they decided that the third page – things she wanted to pay attention to in her own life – would become her goals. Each week Sandra would see how she was attending to improving in certain ways. One was to work at being on time to work. Another, was learning to cope with stress better – in cooperation with her therapist, her doctor, and Mrs. Mullins. There was more.

That became the way that Mrs. Mullins worked with Sandra to work toward an atmosphere of peace and respect, with kindness. Justice called Sandra to discover the truth about what Mrs. Mullin's needs were, as well as how she could learn to cope with her own anxiety and stress. But justice was met with patience, understanding, and love. Life became less worrisome for Sandra. Mrs. Mullins felt more secure. And Sandra stayed long-term as her care-giver.

In Jesus, grace, love and truth meet each other, and in Jesus we come to know God. (John 1:16 – 18)

For Your Reflection

What kind of peace do you seek as you engage in missional monastic ministry?

In what way do you seek truth, and meet truth with love, kindness, and justice?

+ WE WILL SHARE THE REDEEMING, HEALING, CREATIVE LOVE OF GOD IN WORD, DEED, AND PRESENCE IN ORDER TO INVITE OTHERS TO CHRISTIAN DISCIPLESHIP. +

The newly forming community of faith flourishes and grows in number in Jerusalem. However, these followers of the way of Jesus do not stay in the city. Like the early disciples who are sent out into all the world, these believers become scattered in the regions beyond the city, and even further to areas of Palestine near the Mediterranean coast. As they went they lived and shared the good news. (Acts 8:1,4; 11:19 – 26; 13:1 – 2)

God is at work. The purposes of God are resilient. Like an artesian spring, God's presence and purposes spring up in countless ways and in countless places among those who stay in Jerusalem, and through those who are scattered even further to abandoned places of the Empire.

The apostle Peter is mindful of the many who are part of the great diaspora (scattered). As a way of tending the soul of these believers who were now living as aliens and strangers in different and sometimes hostile cultures, Peter writes letters of spiritual direction and encouragement. Saul, who becomes Paul – the apostle to the Gentile world – also writes letters of spiritual guidance and counsel.

So also do John, James, Jude, and the unknown writer of the letter to the Hebrews; all are letters to companion and sustain the community of the scattered. Peter's first letter, which was a point of connection for the scattered believers, will also serve as a point of connection for us -- we who are scattered geographically but are united in call and vision, as we engage in monastic mission.

From Peter, apostle of Jesus Christ –
to God's chosen people
who live as aliens and strangers

s c a t t e r e d

throughout the provinces of
Pontus, Galatia, Cappadocia,
Asia, and Bithynia . . .
relocated to abandoned places of the Empire.

You were chosen
according to the purpose of
God the Father

and were made a holy people
by the Spirit,
to obey Jesus Christ . . .

May grace and peace
be yours in abundance.

1 Peter 1:1 – 2, adapted

Covenant Questions

Witness

Since we last met, in what ways have you:

Been an active agent of reconciliation?

How can we support you in this process?

Engaged in resistance against evil and injustice?

How can we support you in this process?

Shared the redeeming, healing, creative love of God in
word
deed
presence
as an invitation to others to experience the transforming love
of God?

For Your Reflection

In what way do you identify with this early believing community, now
scattered?

What gifts has the Holy Spirit graced you with as you engage in
missional ministry?

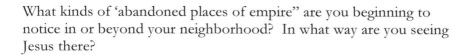

What kinds of 'abandoned places of empire" are you beginning to notice in or beyond your neighborhood? In what way are you seeing Jesus there?

What kind of "push-back" are you encountering?

You may find yourself in an abandoned part of a city or county, where there are very few persons who truly know or understand who you are or what you are doing. You feel the loneliness of being among the scattered.

What kind of "letters" and guidance; what kind of companioning, are a source of encouragement and direction for you?

What else do you sense you need, that is not being provided at this time?

Who can you share this need with? How are you bringing this sense of need to God in prayer? And into conversation with others who do know and understand you – albeit at a distance?

Post Script

Over the last year we have walked many roads together – in the gospel narratives as we tag along with the early disciples, and as we walked the roads of our own local Calcutta. We have also walked the inner road of our own soul – led by the Holy Spirit into places where God is at work, transforming us into those who embody the Rule as we hear the call of Jesus to come – to be with him, and to be sent out. We are learning to walk the road of this primal rhythm, which allows our lives and ministry to be centered around the One who stands at the center of all of life and ministry.

As we live and listen in our own Calcutta, we will also be walking the road with the people to whom Jesus is sending us: hearing their stories, learning their names, coming to know their dreams and desires, even as we understand their needs. Together they and you will be listening to Jesus – the same Jesus who called our name. And we will be inviting them to be with you as you live into this new monastic rule for life, prayer, and missional engagement.

This outward shift will draw us into being contemplatives in action, discerning the presence and action of God as we are with others. Hence, this Post Script is an invitation to cross another threshold into being sent out, just as those early disciples were sent, to embody and announce the Good News of Jesus.

A second work/reflection book, *Listen: Spiritual Discernment for Missional Engagement*, along with *Missional, Monastic, and Mainline*, written by Elaine Heath and Larry Duggins, are designed to companion you as you discern and call a missional team to be come alongside and enter into this missional ministry with you.

In grace, and trust in the One who is with us always, even as we go into all the world.

Wendy J. Miller
Director of Spiritual Formation
Missional Wisdom Foundation
wendyj@missionalwisdom.com
540-421-9725

About the Author

Rev. Wendy Miller is a contemplative story-listener and a transformative instructor. She has a deep love for the narratives which form the biblical mega-story, narratives which offer a doorway for persons to engage with their own life and soul-story, and to encounter God within and behind their storied experience. She currently serves as Director of Spiritual Formation for the Missional Wisdom Foundation and Supervisor of Spiritual Direction for Launch and Lead within the Academy for Missional Wisdom.

She holds a B.A. in Religion and Philosophy from Iowa Wesleyan College, a Masters degree in Church Leadership with a concentration in pastoral care and counseling from Eastern Mennonite Seminary (EMS) in Harrisonburg, VA, and an STM degree in Spiritual Theology and Spiritual Direction from General Theological Seminary in New York City.

Named Professor Emeritus of Spiritual Formation at EMS after teaching spiritual formation, spiritual direction, and supervising training of spiritual directors for 19 years, Wendy continues to nurture the spiritual formation and training of lay persons and clergy in various United Methodist and Mennonite Conferences for the missional ministry of tending the soul of persons/congregation/ communities within and beyond the church. She is an ordained minister within the Virginia Conference of the Mennonite Church.